Praise from readers of *Strai*
Desperate H

GW00750422

Great guidance for my troubled marriage

I started reading this book about a month ago and have noticed a ...... my marriage. The information and examples provided exactly what I was going through. I changed my energy and attitude. I told my wife that I'm going through a process to be a better man and a better husband. The arguing stopped and respect for each other was clearly seen. I utilized what was instructed in the book and I see the difference. It's a process. You have to be patient with it. This book teaches you to be happy within yourself. It's tough, but when I'm down I pick up my phone and read. It grounds me and strengthens me.

My favorite relationship book!

Coming from a person who has countless relationship books, I can wholeheartedly say that this is the one I relate to the most. If you're ready to start the path to becoming the man you want to be in a relationship do yourself a favor and read this book.

Best advice I've ever received on being a husband

Just read the book and you'll begin to see a change immediately. I found things that seemed to be out of nowhere instantly clicking and the benefits of my new mindset pouring over into every other area of my life. Best advice I've ever received on being a husband.

This book flipped a switch for me!

It was a wakeup call that flipped a switch for me. I've made a commitment to myself to control how I act, respond and feel. I am a becoming the man I want to be, treating my wife the way she deserves to be treated. I hope that my marriage improves, but I know that I am improving and that's what matters the most. This book was a life saver!

This book makes me a a better man and husband

I love having Steve's wisdom with me all the time. On the beach, on an airplane, in my car, etc. When I have some time or have nothing to do I can just dive into any chapter and get another AHA moment and learn something new. There is always more to learn when it comes to women and marriage. This book makes me a better man and husband without having to spend hours googling it.

Steve read my mind

Reading this book was as if someone had been following me and writing down everything going on with my marriage and in my mind. Steve found a way inside my head without ever even meeting him. I just finished this book seconds ago and I'm looking forward to going back and reading it again. I must have highlighted half of the book!!!!

STRAIGHT TALK TOOLS FOR THE DESPERATE HUSBAND

How to become a masculine, confident man who can fix his marriage without looking like a controlling a**hole *

*Bonus section for women only

Steve Horsmon

Printed in the United States of America
First Printing, 2020
Goodguys2Greatmen, LLC

ISBN: 978-0-9992039-7-2

Cover Design: Richard Keller

Back Cover Credits:
Hummingbird photo: Backyard-Photography (Jeffrey Schwartz)/Depositphotos.com

Mountain Lion photo: tmild (Tammi Mild)/Depositphotos.com

CONTENTS

Acknowledgments

I want to express my gratitude to the hundreds of men who trust me with their stories, heartbreaks, and courageous internal battles for confidence, emotional strength, and redemption from self-doubt.

If it weren't for these men and our intensely personal coaching conversations, I wouldn't have been able to write this book. Their willingness to be honest, open-hearted, and vulnerable allowed me to look deeper into the modern man's challenges with love, sex, and marriage. They taught me as much as I have taught them. Their personal pain and triumphs are weaved throughout this compilation. This is why, as you read these pieces, you may feel like I've been hiding in the walls of your home. You're not alone, for your story is every man's story.

I want to thank a man named James Motheral. He contacted me out of the blue and said he wanted to help me in any way possible. I was floored and flattered. Together, we came up with the idea to organize about 40 of my most popular articles into a useful reference guide for men trying to salvage their relationships. James did the initial work of reading and organizing the items into chapters.

In his words, "This book will cause you to question, seek further understanding and hopefully realize you aren't alone. It delves into aspects of your psyche and helps you to understand there is somebody who has felt like this before." James is a freelance copywriter at james@pensandpics.com

Thanks to my editor Richard Keller of Wooden Pants Creative Services for believing in this project and giving his kind wisdom and skilled eye to make it better than I could've ever done alone. When he told me he wanted to do the project to help him through his own divorce I knew I had the right man.

Finally, I want to thank my sweetheart and partner who quietly and lovingly supports my obsession to share my passion with the world. At times I was disconnected, distracted, and distraught. What I want for every man is to feel the kind of feminine support, acceptance, and admiration my sweet "Banana" gave to me.

Introduction

I wrote this book for you because nobody else in your life is telling you the truth. Not your dad, your brother, your uncle, your grandfather, or your friends. In fact, those may be the men who try to teach you to play small – to stay in your place.

You may have been taught the damaging myth that a happy wife equals a happy life. You might be under the impression that walking on eggshells, compromising, negotiating, and sacrificing are the keys to a good relationship. This book helps you clear the goo from your eyes and start seeing the truth.

Those myths are the true source of your frustration, fear, and uncertainty. Learning how to be confident in your masculine skin will liberate you. This shall require skills on how to think, speak, and act from a place of inner strength, independence, and self-reliance.

That is your rightful place, despite what you may have learned from men who already succumbed to the pressure to be small.

Our modern-day society is insidiously whittling away men's sense of significance, personal power, and sexual value. The very idea of *masculinity* has taken it on the chin in ways you never saw coming. This emasculation has happened for a number of reasons with a variety of agendas driving it.

Most recently, men have been presented with the notion of *toxic masculinity,* an implication that half of the world was born flawed and requires programming. This process has created armies of zombie men who meander around their lives and relationships with their heads covered. They are confused and frustrated about who they should be and how they should act. They are rocked back on their heels looking for permission to live their life the way they want. Their secret fear is they may never have what they want.

While I don't attempt to deconstruct and analyze this phenomenon in this book, I've made it my mission to reverse it – one man at a time. This is where you come in. You can choose to start living and loving the way you want without fear and without apology. It's a process of taking your balls back.

2

It's your choice to reclaim your right to stand tall and feel proud about who you are. The value you bring and your power to make a positive impact everywhere you go. It's your choice to reclaim the confidence, emotional strength, masculine value, and clarity of purpose that is rightfully yours.

It's how you will learn to stop apologizing for who you are and to find your natural power in being unabashedly honest with your thoughts and unapologetically vulnerable with your feelings. *It is how you can live in your power, create amazing relationships, and honor the passion that runs through your veins.*

I lived for 50 years before someone opened my eyes to a new way of living as a man that feels stronger, clearer, more confident, and *emotionally connected* than at any other time in my life.

My biggest realization is there is nothing new about being this man. He has always lived within me but was spooked into believing he should be kept out of sight. In order to fit in and get my needs met I would play small. I would be nice and please others first. I'd comply and obey. I'd wait for acceptance and nervously yearn for approval.

What my early mentors never told me was that a man's power lies first in his ability to love himself. To know what he expects of himself when nobody is watching defines his character. And knowing what he unapologetically expects *for* himself defines his future.

A man must learn that his sense of well-being, significance, and happiness always comes from *within*– not outside – of himself. Self-reliance and the ability to self-validate form the foundation of true self-esteem.

It's only from this place of inner strength where a man can properly chart his course, make clear decisions, and set unmovable boundaries. And it's only from the place of healthy self-reliance that a man can lead himself and create passionate connections with others without playing games.

I spent a lifetime struggling in the world of men, women, and relationships because nobody told me there was another way. Throughout childhood, high school, college, career, and 28 years of marriage I carried a dirty little secret: I didn't really know who I was or what I stood for.

I didn't feel confident in speaking up for what I wanted because I didn't actually know what I wanted. I was highly trained in the art of pleasing others and making others happy, all in the secret pursuit of having them like me back. Maybe, just maybe, if I pleased everyone around me they would provide approval and the sense of significance and belonging I needed.

This path led to the realization that I had to change. I had to stop waiting for positive changes to come into my life and create something new that would come out of me. It hit me like a ton of bricks!

I realized I had total control of what comes out of me and how my life goes. The response to my circumstances was all that mattered. When I acted from a place of clarity and purpose my circumstances changed.

I took a deep dive into the study of masculinity, femininity, and sexuality. I studied the powerful psychological, biological, sociological, and philosophical works of great men and women who were and are engaged in the same battle as me. Then I began to meet and work with powerful men to learn more about this journey and how to stay focused and strong.

Eventually, I created my own business called **Goodguys2Greatmen, LLC.** This became my launching pad for a new career of serving men like myself. These are sensitive, intelligent, compassionate, romantic, and passionate men who want to live bigger lives. They want to rebuild their manly mojo – a combination of emotional strength, confidence, and clarity. They want to leave the mediocrity of negotiation, compromise, and sacrifice of everything that is important to them.

And they want to make a bigger impact, create more passion and wealth … and leave a legacy.

In 2013, I began my professional coaching business. I've coached men all around the world and have learned the common struggles that bind us. With over 100 published articles, 200 newsletters, and 100 produced videos, I've developed a sense of what men most need in their daily lives.

With this insight, I decided to create this book for you. It's a collection of the most impactful articles I've written, and they have been divided into specific themes for you. I share powerful stories and concepts with you. Some of these may challenge your current thinking. At times, you may feel both scared and inspired.

Eventually, a surge of self-confidence and self-respect will emerge. From there you may feel the rush of overwhelming opportunity with a twinge of anxiety on how to take your next steps.

You will wonder why nobody told you these things when you were 18 years old. Also, you may have a few epiphanies that make you shake your head just like I did when I began this work.

You may get angry at some parts. Angry at those who "programmed" you this way, and angry at yourself for allowing it to happen. This is a good thing!

Anger is a sign you're prepared to take the steering wheel of your life and reclaim what is rightfully yours – confidence, clarity, courage, and a sense of direction and purpose in your life and relationship. You're about to begin leading yourself so you can lead others and create what you want instead of simply reacting to what you've been handed.

You will make some big decisions and push toward uncomfortable "edges" you've been taught to stay away from. This will create anxiety and uncertainty in those around you who don't understand the transformation you're undergoing. You'll learn to be comfortable in other people's discomfort and feel liberated as you let go of worrying about what others think of you, what you want, and where you want to go.

The best thing a man can do is surround himself with people who challenge and encourage him. This book is meant to do just that. But you can't simply rely on books. You need *initiated men* in your life who believe in you. Men who boldly tell you what you need to hear – not just what you want to hear.

Your life depends on it.

How to Read This Book

This is a reference book – not a novel.

You can and should skip around at will.

I pulled together a set of 40 articles I originally published on The Good Men Project website. These articles have been categorized into chapters that focus on different aspects of men, women, relationships, marriage, communication, confidence, and masculinity. In keeping with the theme of straight talk tools, the chapter names are automobile maintenance metaphors for the different stages of your relationship.

Some parts will resonate in ways that make you think I've been hiding out in your bedroom or kitchen. Other parts may not mean anything at all. Men who've never spoken to me have said these articles changed their mindset, their relationships, and their life.

There's a lot of gold to mine here if you're willing to act on your own,

Your job is to use this work in a way that feels right for you. Many of the original articles have long strings of reader comments which are sometimes more helpful than the article itself. To see these comments, just google the title of the article and my last name.

Finally, I want you to consider this as the beginning of your journey. As you read and process the information, and your emotions, you may be moved to dive deeper. Send your thoughts, feelings, and questions directly to steve@goodguys2greatmen.com. I will personally respond to your email.

If you reach a point where you believe you are ready for real action and commitment, I invite you to contact us for a free discovery call to discuss your situation, talk about your goals, and give you some guidance you can use to immediately improve things!

Chapter 1

THE OIL CHANGE – IMPROVE YOUR CONFIDENCE BY CHANGING YOUR THINKING

> "Some of the biggest challenges in relationships come from the fact that most people enter a relationship in order to get something: they're trying to find someone who's going to make them feel good. In reality, the only way a relationship will last is if you see your relationship as a place that you go to give, and not a place that you go to take."
> ~ANTHONY ROBBINS

I don't use the phrases "Be a man," "Man up," or "Real Man." I don't believe they give any clarity to what true masculine strength and confidence looks like. They are typically used as insults and attempts to emasculate individuals or a group of men. In these articles, I explain the energy of a strong, confident man and how it looks and feels to him.

Our purpose in developing strength and confidence is to never dominate or control others but to achieve a level of self-control and self-reliance so we can lead ourselves first. We always start with ourselves. We have nothing to give unless we are clear about who we are, what we stand for and the value we offer.

Evolving Men Have Two Choices, And One of Them Will Ruin Your Life

Does the world seem to just happen to you, or do you happen to the world?

This is not a scientific discussion, so don't expect a lot of mumbo-jumbo about Darwin and survival of the fittest. I have only one point to make, and it's a warning about your future. Yes, I can predict it with stunning accuracy.

How? I've got good data. I see it every day.

I see men who achieve massive clarity, confidence, and strength in their lives when just one switch flips in their mindset. And I see other men who wallow in unhappiness, frustration, and self-pity when they can't find that switch.

The one factor that determines which man you will be is the answer to this question ...

Do you typically react to your environment, or do you expect your environment to react to you?

Evolved Man Type I

This man is a classic evolutionary example. He sees the world and his life as a whirlwind of variables that happen to him. His default mode of reaction is defensiveness and quiet submission. Changes in his life occur without warning and without permission. His only option is to adapt. He accepts the pressures of environmental flux as his fate.

This pisses him off. He agonizes over every decision in his life as if the consequences could ruin him. He decides it's safer to not decide at all. He believes his very survival depends on his ability to quietly bend to the will of the world.

This belief will ruin his life in every respect.

Some call him disadvantaged. Some call him unlucky. He agrees with them.

Evolved Man Type II

This man is a renegade. He believes evolution is proactive, not passive. The world doesn't happen to him. He happens to the world.

He expects the world to bend to his will, his dreams, and his intention to create his own happiness. He doesn't wait for change to happen to him because he is too busy creating changes of his own. He sees everything he does as a simple response – a course correction – on the way to his destiny.

Changes in his life are merely steppingstones, not barriers. His only option is to use those obstacles for improving his game and becoming wiser. The pressure of uncertainty is his lifeblood, his fuel.

Every decision he makes is less important than his response to the consequences of that decision. With this mindset, he moves swiftly. It appears effortless to the less informed.

He believes his very survival depends on his ability to make decisions, learn quickly, and keep moving toward his goal. This belief improves his life in every respect.

Some call him brave. Other just call him lucky.

He knows differently. He can't explain it because they wouldn't get it.

Which Will You Choose?

You can choose to be Evolved Man Type I or Type II.

Many men suffocate themselves with books, articles, videos, and audio training modules all designed to awaken them. They ride the rollercoaster through the peaks and valleys of personal development, spiritual growth, and self-actualization. It's like brain candy – sweet and satisfying. Contentment wraps them in her arms.

Then their stomachs growl, hungry for more. They are faced with a decision. They must take a stand. Or maybe some action is required on their part.

At this point, Type I men return to the libraries of shelf-help hell for another serving from the all-you-can-eat dessert bar. They may attend just one more webinar, workshop, or retreat. Anything to avoid a decision. Anything to avoid the risk of the unknown. It's easier to let the world happen to them.

The Type II man also feasts at the personal growth buffet, but he knows when to stop. He finds his comfort in the certainty and momentum of forward motion. His books are tools for action, and he knows wisdom is always the reward for action.

The world quietly bends to his will, his dreams, and his intention.

Building More Intimacy Handling Conflict Like a Man

How to be a prize-winning communicator in a relationship.

I recently read about a study on the LiveScience website titled "Women Prize Men Who Try to Understand Their Emotions." My first reaction was, "Well, no kidding!" But as I read a little further and understood the nature of the study, one conclusion stood out. It is a counter-intuitive reality that men need to understand. Women value a man who expresses either positive or negative emotion in response to conflict.

The Harvard Medical School study researcher, Shiri Cohen, reported, "The fact their partner is experiencing any emotion, even a negative one, is still good news to women. This is consistent with what is known about the dissatisfaction women often experience when their male partner becomes emotionally withdrawn and disengaged in response to conflict."

As a coach for men, I often have discussions with them about improving intimacy. Men want both emotionally and physically intimate connections to feel positive about their spouse and their relationship. The two biggest reasons men are unable to establish these connections are:

1. Failure to establish themselves as attractive and authentic men of value and principles
2. Failure to develop the confidence and personal leadership skills necessary to guide their relationship toward intimacy.

A critical part of establishing yourself as an attractive authentic man is how you handle conflict with your partner. A woman simply cannot feel attracted to a man who handles conflict poorly or immaturely. Simply put – when a man properly responds to conflict with his lady, he can become significantly more attractive to her.

Many men believe withdrawing or disengaging leaves her in neutral regarding his attractiveness. Not true. This is a tremendous insult and extremely unattractive. A repeated pattern of this behavior can spell disaster for the relationship. Always remember, you have a choice to respond to conflict instead of reacting to it. A man who chooses to immaturely react to conflict does the following:

> **Choices To Immaturely React To Conflict**
> - Avoid all discussion or walk away from the conflict and isolate himself.
> - Act indifferent toward her emotions as if he is above the whole matter.
> - Dismiss her feelings as totally irrational or illogical.
> - Refuse to voice his opinions or show any emotions for fear of her reactions.
> - Lash out with an unbridled anger and accusatory tone.

So, what are we supposed to do? How do we act? How do we build or maintain attractiveness in the face of conflict?

The answer is to realize that properly responding within your masculine frame is a gift we give to ourselves first. We can validate our own value when we directly face conflict with confidence. We affirm our values when we choose to treat others fairly and respectfully. And we confirm our own principles when we stand up for ourselves and express our opinions without apology.

A natural result of a man who chooses to behave differently is increased attractiveness. This is what makes you the prize for your lady. The man you were meant to be chooses to proactively address conflict because it is who he is.

Committed Actions For A Proactive Man Under Pressure

Calmly faces conflict head-on. He responds like and adult and doesn't react like a teenager. He looks at her eyes.

He listens actively to her words. He is comfortable and confidently 100% present with her in the moment.

Tells her he wants to understand her feelings. He treats the conflict as important and valid. He says this out loud and means it. He does not minimize her feelings or point of view.

He does not pull the logic card and call her irrational. He knows conflict and stress produce emotions. He doesn't react to them or defend himself while he listens. Her emotions cannot and should not be reasoned away.

He is clear on where he stands. He doesn't have to pretend to agree with her if he doesn't. Without defensiveness or judgment, he states his case clearly and without apology.

He's authentic and speaks from a place of love and respect. He wants her to feel this energy and to know that it is true.

He discusses options to address the issue and accepts responsibility for his part in the solution. He doesn't accept undeserved blame or personal attacks.

He shows anger and emotion without throwing a tantrum or making personal attacks. He doesn't initiate disrespectful behavior or language and does not accept it from anyone else.

When you choose to develop these skills and this frame of mind in your relationships it is not to manipulate or control anyone. You will discover that it is the only way to lead your life with clarity and confidence. These skills apply beautifully in your parenting and your career relationships as well. It is simply the man you are meant to be.

How to Warm Up Your Unaffectionate Wife

Basic attributes of husbands who get all the affection they want.

In this article, I share the three most important attributes I've identified in husbands – and men in general – who get all the affection they want.

This is about the basic foundation of a man who takes the lead in *creating* what he wants. He knows beyond any doubt that creation requires him to *be* what he wants. He happens to the world. He doesn't wait for the world to happen to him.

While there are dozens of other ingredients that add to a thriving, affectionate relationship, I believe a man will struggle no matter what without this trio of attributes.

The Three Basics Attributes of the Affectionately Satisfied Man

Basic Attribute 1: He Shamelessly Gives Affection And He Means It

This doesn't mean he constantly gushes over her with smothering attention, compliments, and touches. He is shameless in that he knows his attention, compliments and touches are genuine. He gives these things from a clear intention of love, honor, and respect, and he has no concern for what others think about his affectionate nature.

He doesn't give his affection and then look over his shoulder for a positive reaction. There's no hidden agenda for showing his appreciation generously. He isn't the least bit ashamed to give her – or anyone else – these things because he knows they have value. He knows this because he is a man of value, which leads me to number two.

Basic Attribute 2: He Doesn't Feel Entitled to Affection – He Creates

He is spiritually grounded in the *certainty* that people are meant to share love and affection. This is not negotiable for him. He will live a life full of affection – period. He doesn't feel *entitled* to affection from any particular person – he simply knows he *deserves* a life full of affection. And he is unashamed to make this known to everyone in his life.

Does this create pressure on those he invites into his life? Yes, but he won't apologize for it because it's simply his truth. Due to his shameless willingness to give affection, he attracts and spends time with those who share his values. He believes in his worth as a man and husband. He chooses only to be in a relationship that values mutual respect while consciously and continually fostering affection.

Basic Attribute 3: He Expects More From Himself And Others

The affectionately satisfied man doesn't shy away from having expectations. He is under no illusion that it's rude, wrong, or controlling to have high expectations of and *for* himself. He doesn't tolerate antagonistic energy from within and he doesn't tolerate it from others.

His wife is aware of that. She is with him because she also has high expectations. She enjoys being called to her higher self and vice-versa.

Neither of them play in the shallow end of life or marriage. They call each other to go deeper. It can be an uncomfortable edge to push

– always expecting more depth, vulnerability, and connection. But they keep their standards high because that's the life they believe they were meant to live.

What If Only ONE Person Participates?

This is the obvious question.

What do you do if you feel like you are the only one trying to create the relationship you want? What do you do if you find yourself in a committed, long-term, romantic relationship – including marriage – where your expectations for the affectionate life you want are not fulfilled?

It's a very personal choice, and I don't believe there is one clear answer for everyone.

But in my experience, the first three questions are harder to answer. That's why we jump straight to question four. It allows us to skip past our own accountability.

> **The Questions To Ask Yourself**
>
> Have I *consistently* avoided the mistakes that antagonize the problem? If so, for how long?
>
> Have I established the foundation of an affectionately satisfied person? If not, what am I waiting for?
>
> Have I set high self-expectations? Have I made my desires and expectations clear? If not, why?
>
> If creating a loving, genuinely affectionate relationship is one of my top values, why would I choose to share my life with someone who doesn't share those values?

I've discovered that if I devote my time and focus on the first questions, I don't need to ask number four.

I already know the answer to that.

She Said I'm an "Amazing Man." Why Didn't My Wife See That?

Sometimes husbands become amazing men after divorce. Why can't we achieve that beforehand?

"I'll probably never be able love anyone like I loved Jessica," Paul told me a few weeks after the divorce from his wife of 18 years."

His last year of marriage was an exhausting struggle as he watched Jessica pull further and further away until she finally moved out.

"We can still be friends, can't we?" she would say, and Paul grabbed onto that possibility thinking it could be his only chance to win her back. They would spend weekends together camping or hiking with the kids. She would let him kiss her. They even had incredible sex one evening, even though Jessica said she was no longer attracted to him.

And then she would pull away again -- detaching. Acting lost and confused. Paul knew she saw other people. Why did she keep him on this tether? Why was she playing games with his heart? Why did he let her? Why did he allow himself to be emotionally jerked around?

Because he loved her. Plain and simple. And he would probably never be able to love anyone like her again.

Their trial friendship ended in a couple of months, and they numbly navigated through their divorce, dividing money, cars, pets, and time with their kids.

Paul didn't quite know what hit him or where he was headed. But he had been doing quite a bit of work and self-study and he knew one thing: He was going to be okay. Better than okay.

Fast Forward One Year

Paul was committed to learn something from the pain and confusion of his divorce. He spent a solid year diving deep into this project. He focused on getting crystal clear on what he believed about himself, relationships, and women. His self-imposed standards and his boundaries needed to be defined. Paul wanted to hold himself accountable for operating at a higher level as a man and for surrounding himself with more positive, supportive people. He decided to choose happiness over regret.

The pain and guilt he felt became motivation to learn more about why some "nice guys" seem to have a pattern of difficult relationships with women. He now recognized the unhealthy behaviors he used to manipulate Jessica and how he heavily relied on her for his happiness.

Paul wanted more self-confidence in how he saw the world and how he showed up in his emotions and his actions. He studied and finally became clear about the source of his self-respect and well-being. He developed a personal spirituality around his sense of purpose and "deservingness." This made him feel more deliberate in his thoughts and his decisions.

And he learned about vulnerability and empathy. For the first time, he clearly saw how Jessica's personal challenges and choices were more about her than about him. He saw and felt her experience in the marriage. His divorce really wasn't all about him, and that gave him a huge sense of relief and calm feeling of compassion for her journey.

Paul resolved to stop treading so lightly in life. He had been playing small and knew he was capable of so much more. He wanted out of his comfort zone and to push the edges of his fears. He wanted to feel bolder and to take more risks. And so, he did. He pushed forward with more confidence in himself, his work, and his new interest in dating.

"This Woman Blew Me Away!"

Paul began going on a few dates to test the waters. He agonized over writing his profile and finally decided to just put down the simple, raw truth about who he was, what he believed and what he brought to the party. He was unapologetic about his desire for deeper connections with women and was bold in his expectations for honesty and authenticity.

After three uneventful dates, he met another woman for a fourth attempt. He later told me, "This woman blew me away." Here is the story in his words.

"We met for drinks on a weeknight at 6 p.m., and literally the next thing we knew they were closing at midnight. We had no idea. We hugged and went our separate ways. Halfway home she sent me a message that she had an amazing time and smiled all the way home and couldn't wait to see me again.

"What a feeling. We arranged a second date to dinner. We had reservations at 6:30, again on a weeknight. We got our meal and a bottle of wine, and again they came to our table and told us they had closed a half hour ago and really needed us to leave. She again texted me while I was driving home telling me what an amazing man I am and she couldn't wait to see me again.

"Man, I have to tell you, I have never had a woman make me feel the way she does. One clue, when I was over at her place one night for dinner, she showed me an article on her phone that she had been reading and wanted my opinion. It was an article on the site! That impressed the hell out of me that she was reading things about men's needs and desires.

"We seem to have an unbelievable connection, and it feels amazing. She tells me that she can't believe that she found a man like me who allows her to be the strong, independent woman that she is (she is a lawyer and owns her own law firm and was a captain in the Air Force) but also makes her feel completely free to let her guard down and be vulnerable.

"She said she never had a man that she could rely on or trust. She says I make her feel like a woman. It's been pretty amazing so far, and I'm really looking forward to seeing where it goes."

Why Couldn't I Have This With My Wife?

Like most men I know (including me) who reach this point after divorce, we ask ourselves *"Why couldn't we achieve this kind of connection with our wife?"*

The best answer I can give is, "Because we were not yet the type of man who achieves that kind of stuff with women."

I wasn't ready. Paul wasn't ready.

Developing personal confidence and clarity takes work. Choosing to look inward and discover your own value, self-expectations, and boundaries takes balls.

Sometimes in marriage we lack the motivation, ambition, or courage to develop our masculine operating principles and boldly live in ways which honor them. It may take the pain of divorce to finally open our eyes and hearts and step out of our comfort zone. *And it's often our fear of divorce which paralyzes us and keeps us from acting before it's too late.*

Can this work be done inside the context of a struggling marriage? Absolutely. It just might be the thing which lifts both of you into a higher level of relationship and fuels a "second marriage" effort. Other times, it will be the thing which brings you clarity for the need to end the marriage.

No matter what outcome occurs, you can't avoid doing the work. And if you're doing the work for the right reasons, it will be the outcome that is *supposed* to happen.

Learn Tarzan's Secret – "Jane Pretty When Mad"

If Tarzan can figure this out, so can you.

I had to laugh out loud at something a guy told me the other day.

Allen was feeling defeated about his interactions with his wife. Without knowing it, he gave me the perfect example of the kind of results men tell me they want most. If they could just figure out how to act more like Tarzan, they would feel so much better about life in general.

Allen: It happened again last night, Steve. She was angry about something at work involving her boss and another coworker. She kept ranting and then looked at me and said, "Why do you guys have to be such assholes to women?"

Me: What did you say?

Allen: I took the bait again, and I said something stupid about how women are irrational and impossible to talk to.

Me: Then what?

Allen: Then we got into a nasty, hour-long argument about feminism, misogyny, and equal rights.

Me: Sounds fun. What would you do if you could have a do-over?

Allen: You know those old Tarzan movies? There's a scene where Tarzan and Jane are in the jungle and Jane gets really mad at him for something, I don't know what. But he just smiles at her and is totally unaffected. Then he just says, "Jane pretty when mad."

Me: What did Jane do?

Allen: She just rolled her eyes and they went on about their jungle day. Damn, I wish I could have the peace of mind and confidence to say things like that and be like that!

Me: (LOL) Don't we all, Allen. Let's talk about how Tarzan got there. You can do this – you just don't know it yet.

I told Allen about my experiences reacting to my wife. Like a lot of guys, I had a hair-trigger when it came to any implication of disappointment or disapproval from her. "If she was angry, she must be angry with me," I figured. I must have screwed up somehow, and now I had to figure out why and how to fix it fast. That normally included a boyish reaction, an insult, an argument – and then the silent treatment.

If my wife were really upset about her boss, her mother, or me I would react by recoiling and preparing a defensive retort. I internalized her anger as an indictment of me and my status as a "really good guy" everyone else seemed to like just fine! Resentment filled my veins.

That's exactly where Allen was with his wife. And the thought of saying, "Jane pretty when mad," was nowhere on his radar.

What Does "Jane pretty when mad" Look Like?

A client of mine, Bill, learned how to turn his tendency to react to his wife into a "Jane pretty when hungry" response. His wife had a habit of coming home from work in a tense and irritated mood. She would immediately start complaining about everything. It was so predictable and annoying to Bill that he would usually get into a spiteful argument with her about something.

Then he figured it out. His wife was always coming home hungry, and, as a result, this always made her agitated. So, Bill decided to make some fun snacks they could share together when she got home from work.

He said, "You should have seen the look on her face when I just casually put out the snacks and asked her about her day." Bill engineered his own "Jane pretty when mad" response and no longer worried about her moods upon arriving home.

Ladies can do this for us, too. It happened for me in my kitchen at 7 a.m. Except that it was more of a "Tarzan sexy when mad" moment.

I was sleepily making my sweetie a cup of coffee with our Keurig one cup, magic machine, pain-in-the-ass … umm … coffee maker. Standing there barefoot in my fleece jammies I heard the machine burp, hiss, and then erupt hot water and coffee grinds all over the counter and the floor. I felt boiling water between my toes as the cat jumped into the middle of the mess. I tossed the kitty out of harm's way and just yelled, "F*ck! Goddam piece of crap!"

My "Jane" puttered down the hallway with a toothbrush in her mouth, humming some damn song that was in her head. She shuffled up to me, opened her arms, and muffled through her foamy lips, "You want a hug?" She helped clean up, made a comment about cleaning the machine this weekend, patted my ass, and went back to her business with the hair dryer.

To me it felt like, "Tarzan sexy when mad." And I liked it.

FYI, ladies – every guy who read that last part is now shaking their head thinking, "Damn, what a mythical creature."

For men, this is exactly what the "Jane pretty when mad" energy is all about. It's about a calm, deliberate, and unrattled masculine gift of acceptance. It's about not following the drama and negative energy of the moment.

It's about assuming the *best* about your partner – that her anger is not about you. It's not personal. There is no reason to react to her anger with defensiveness or boyish insecurity.

"Jane pretty when mad" is any response you can muster from a place of self-confidence, presence, and love.

This Is Really About You – Not Jane

When we start doing personal development work inside our relationships, we need to check our motivations. Sometimes we choose to learn a new mindset and tools for the wrong reasons.

We want "Jane" to like us. We want her to swing with us. We bring bananas so she gives us crazy, hot monkey love to make us feel good about ourselves.

Jane not like your hidden agenda, and neither should you.

Why? If you want to be more like Tarzan, you also need to know his secret: Tarzan very happy with Tarzan and not *need* Jane to give him anything.

Tarzan is so comfortable, confident, and at peace in his own skin that he only needs a loincloth. He doesn't rely on Jane to make him feel like Tarzan but she likes to.

He doesn't need Jane to give him hugs, kisses, and crazy hot monkey love. Nevertheless, she likes to.

Tarzan knows he has options. There are other Janes in the jungle if his one doesn't like him the way he is.

Yet, every day, Tarzan chooses Jane and offers her his consistent presence, support, and strength. He's independent but dependable. He sprinkles in some fun and humor in there, too.

That's just how Tarzan rolls. And Jane like that.

I received an email from Allen a few days later. He had been practicing his Tarzan mojo – calm, present and unrattled. Here's what he said:

"I am amazed how my not reacting turned out to be such a positive thing. But, boy, in my mind I was definitely having a reaction. My wife had forgotten about her [snarky comment] in a couple of minutes and her tone turned normal and the morning turned out fine."

How to Stop Depending on Her and Start Attracting Her Again

How to improve your independence and start attracting her at the same time.

Many husbands and boyfriends these days are operating to a dangerous set of rules. I didn't see this and I didn't escape this reality until much later in life. Now that my eyes are clear and my head is on straight, I want to help you before it's too late.

The Dangerous Rules
The rules many men were raised with.

- If momma ain't happy, then nobody's happy.
- Don't rock the boat.
- Walking on eggshells is what good boys do.
- Happy wife equals a happy life.
- Whatever you do, do not piss her off.
- Make sure you get a kitchen pass.
- Your needs are always second.
- All women are emotional. Deal with it, suck it up, and learn to apologize.

Why These Are Dangerous Rules?
Each one puts you in a second-fiddle frame of mind. In turn, they make you do dangerous things.

- Tread lightly and tentatively in every conversation.
- Act with caution and uncertainly when it comes to decisions.
- Constantly seek approval with validation.
- Follow her rules up and down, like you're on a roller coaster.
- Overreact every time you think you did something good and get no credit.
- Argue with her about things that need no argument.
- Get defensive and justify yourself each time she seems unhappy.
- Stay in a perpetual pissy state of resentment and indignation.

What Happens When You Do Dangerous Things?
The second-fiddle frame of makes your relationship incredibly frustrating and stressful.

- You feel like crap – angry crap.
- She finds you indescribably unattractive and unsexy.
- You want to avoid her and hide out.
- She wants space from you.
- You complain about lack of intimacy.
- She says she doesn't need another kid to take care of.
- You go to work mad and underperform.
- She sleeps with her back to you.

How To Stop Being Dependent

The short story above has become an epidemic of sorts. As I mentioned, I finally got my vaccine. The cure to this cycle of despair lies in one incredibly elusive character trait ... self-reliance. Without it, we are doomed to depend on the feedback, permission, and endorsement of everyone else but ourselves. And in your relationship, lacking self-reliance may very likely be the culprit behind your frustrations and dissatisfaction. It's also normally tied to feelings of neglect, emasculation, and disrespect.

Self-reliance is the trait of being able to self-endorse, self-validate, and self-approve. I help men learn how to earn these stripes through action – one step at a time.

Entry-Level Actions You Must Take To Be Self-Reliant

- Make a non-negotiable list of your self-expectations independent of anyone else's opinion. What do you demand of yourself without input from anyone else?
- Make a non-negotiable list of what you expect for yourself. What do you demand for the environment and relationship you want to live in?
- Make a non-negotiable list of the specific boundaries you have for your own behavior and for those you choose to include in your life. Decide that you shall hold yourself accountable and stand up for yourself.
- Understand that no man is born self-reliant. Most of us slowly and surely give up our independence and learn to measure our value, significance, and worthiness through the eyes of others. This can easily be reversed with proper desire, focus, and commitment.

What Happens When You Become Self-Reliant?

When men learn to become self-reliant, I hear them say things like:

"Holy crap, this is so liberating!"

Or,

"I had no idea how dependent I had become and how it was making me, and her, crazy."

Or,

"I feel so damn confident now, it's funny to see her chasing me for a change."

I don't make this stuff up. These are real words men use.

It's so simple, yet so difficult to see when you're in the chaos and pain of a relationship.

Self-reliant people wake up happier and go to bed more content. They don't think of being alone as loneliness.

Self-reliant people tend to talk more clearly and boldly without worrying about reactions or judgement.

Self-reliant people trust their own judgement, are more decisive and they don't seek approval for who they are.

And most importantly … they're not assholes.

They find the only way to truly love, truly be present, truly empathize, and truly support another is when they don't need anything from them.

Chapter 2

TUNING THE ROUGH ENGINE – COMMON CAUSES OF UNHAPPINESS AND DISCONTENT

> "Today I will stop trying to control my relationships. I will participate at a reasonable level and let the other person do the same. I can let go, knowing that the relationship will find its own life or not and I don't have to do all the work ... only my share."
> ~MELODY BEATTIE

The "good guy" husband is the kind who tries to make her happy – no matter what. He's been sold on the "happy wife – happy life" myth and is just about killing himself trying to keep her happy. In the end, it's the very source of his problems. I have a PhD in people-pleasing and discovered the pitfalls in this mindset.

"Good guys" typically lack self-respect and have a hard time setting boundaries. In the end, they wind up feeling disrespected, ignored, and unappreciated. The only way to reverse these feelings is to learn how to respect yourself first. These articles are focused on helping you do just that.

How Good Guys Can Become Chronically Unhappy Husbands

The common hidden agenda afflicting many good guys who wind up as unhappy husbands.

Every chronically unhappy husband I work with battles a very common affliction. It's his mindset. The way he thinks about his role and his life as a married man needs what I call a mojo makeover. * And until he decides to buckle down and focus on changing his self-sabotaging thoughts he will continue feeling what he's feeling and getting what he's getting.

Traits Of Chronically Unhappy Husbands

- He will keep trying to "make her happy." He will constantly worry about what she thinks of him.
- He'll continue doing anything and everything to get her attention, gain her approval, and feel her appreciation.
- He'll jump through more and more hoops each day, so she might give him what he wants.
- In his mind, he's been a really "good husband." The best kind. The caring, attentive, provider kind.
- Everything would be fine if she would just acknowledge that and validate him.

---

*Obviously, mojo makeovers are equally essential for chronically unhappy wives. There are many resources out there for that.

Why Good Guy Doesn't Always Equal Good Husband

A client I'll call Kevin told me that his wife just blurted out one day, "Just because you're a good guy doesn't make you a good husband!"

"What the hell does that mean?" he asked me.

Kevin is like thousands of unhappily married men who aren't getting what they want from marriage. He's a powerful and competent man at work. He is highly respected and appreciated by his co-workers and his clients. He's decisive, quick witted, funny, and persuasive. He has a tight group of friends and considers himself a caring, sensitive, and conscious guy.

After hearing how he operated in his marriage, I could pinpoint the problem.

Kevin is used to getting what he wants. His relationship skills outside of his marriage are effective at engineering the outcomes he desires. He knows how to get people to like him and get their agreement with doing the things he wants them to do.

Outside of his relationship it seems to work pretty well. His wife knows this about him. She sees how effective he is at work and how people gravitate toward his confident and assertive nature. He is patient and kind with everyone ...

Except her.

She doesn't respond to his manipulations and subtle games of getting his needs met, and that pisses him off. He not only wants her to want him but he also needs it more than anything. While he gets his validation-bucket filled easily at work, it's not so easy at home. He relies heavily on his wife to make him feel okay daily about his masculine value and his sexual worthiness. His need for external validation from her is insatiable. His subsequent dark moods, angry outbursts, and seething resentment create a predictable pattern in their relationship.

He wants to know how to change her. How can he make her more appreciative and desirous of him? Shouldn't she want to make him happy?

Being A Happy Man First – Happy Husband Second

Kevin's personal challenge is hardly rare these days. I didn't escape it either.

It's the mindset and belief that we are dependent on outside validation and acceptance to be happy men. It's the trap of holding others hostage for making us feel whole and worthy. It makes us resent them for not filling those needs. as a result, they resent us for being given an utterly impossible assignment.

I regarded women, sex, and marriage as oases from which my sense of well-being could be filled anytime I needed. Feeling like a happy man required me to be dependent on feminine approval, sexual surrender, and unconditional commitment.

Perhaps like me, you are the product of a few generations of men who have become experts in the art of pleasing women and using relationships with them as the wellspring for your sense of masculine purpose and value. This is a habit we develop early on when we find easy targets in mothers, aunts and teachers who are all too willing to let us drink from their generous fountain of approval and "attaboys." This is exacerbated by the absence of strong, masculine role models to teach us another way.

So, what now? We're decades past our formative years and still confused on what to do next.

The only possible way to achieve true happiness inside our relationships is to take responsibility for learning what it truly means to be a happy man outside our relationships.

First things first. This means we must deliberately and mercifully release those we've held accountable for our happiness. I don't mean leave them. I mean release the pressure from them. Both of you will massively lighten your load and feel a wave of relief. As we take our own initiative we will feel the departure of our clinging inner boy who has feared this day for some time now.

The Key To Becoming A Happy Man

Learning to become a happy man is your paramount mission. Nothing else is more important, and nothing else will improve your life more dramatically.

Men first approach me with this problem when their intimate, committed, and romantic relationship has hit a wall. It's in these relationships where we first feel the intense pain of masculine inadequacy and powerlessness. It's the first time our lack of emotional self-reliance is so vulnerably exposed, and our women don't waste much time testing that sensitive underbelly. They can't and won't accept our demands for attention and validation like our mothers and teachers did. It's actually a favor if you can get yourself to see the beauty in it. I know how tough that can be.

The key to becoming a happy man inside our relationships is to learn that we already have everything we need inside of us to be happy. We have the ability, imagination, and initiative to create whatever we want and to become whatever we want. Happiness comes from choosing to manipulate our own circumstances – not the people around us. If we no longer want to be an unhappy man who seeks well-being and worthiness from others, we can change that circumstance. If we want to feel more confident in ourselves and our sexual value we can change that circumstance. And if we want to build emotional self-reliance and a sense of personal power we can change that circumstance.

This is totally achievable when we develop more clarity around our personal values and self-expectations. We must reprogram our confused notions about masculine value, women, and sex. Instead, we must accept responsibility for believing in our own self-worth and develop the confidence to stand strong in what we expect from ourselves and for ourselves.

Is it significantly more work to do that than to demand others to do it for us? Yes, but which one creates the real results and lasting happiness we want for our next 30 years?

Owning our happiness and facing our fears is a scary proposition. Fear of change and the unknown is what freezes us in place.

Why Hummingbird Husbands Get No Lovin'

**Can you relate to these traits of the "hummingbird husband?"
I can.**

Hummingbirds are nervous little fellers. Uncertain and twitchy.
They don't trust anyone or anything. They're always questioning
and anxious as hell hovering for their turn at the feeder. With a
flying heart rate around 1000 beats per minute, I wonder why they
don't explode in mid-air.

Can you relate? I can.

The Guaranteed Libido Killer

I'm a leading authority on the "hummingbird husband." I was
one for many years, and I can now spot it easily in the men I work
with. It's a syndrome that's sure to leave you feeling agitated with
yourself. Furthermore, it's a guaranteed libido killer in all wives.
One hundred percent of them. Did I mention I'm an expert?

We're not bad husbands. Actually, we're really super guys. Perhaps a little overly involved, but we mean well ... maybe. We're just being attentive – possibly too attentive. We just want to know what's going on.

We want to know what she's doing, where she's going, who she's talking to, who she's texting. We want to know what she's buying, why she needs it, why she's late, and how could she possibly not know she was driving on a flat tire? Doesn't she know that will ruin a tire?

Hummingbird husbands ask a lot of questions and rarely make simple statements. Rapid fire innocent inquiries are our specialty. It's exhausting for both of us.

We have our dirty little secret about our overwhelming concern for her well-being. When we keep asking/ "Are you okay? What's the matter? Did I do something wrong? Why are you mad? How are you doing?" what we're really asking is ... "Am I okay?"

Am I Okay? Am I Okay? Am I Okay?

In my hovering days, this was the underlying question behind most of my questions: "Am I okay? Are we okay? Do you still love me? Do you still want me?"

It's embarrassing as hell to admit I was that guy for some time. I sought continual reassurance everything was okay. That *I* would be okay. Insecurity sucks, and it's magnified about 100 times toward the end of a marriage. It can eat a man alive.

I was a typical hummingbird husband. To the outside world I was a model of calmness and stability. At work and social situations I was Mr. Cool. It was *not* an act. I really was Mr. Cool. But I could never figure out where Mr. Cool went when I was in my own house.

Like I said, insecurity sucks, and it seems to be triggered the most in our romantic relationships – inside our own home.

Yeah, I'm Okay

If you can relate to any part of the hummingbird husband's story, I want you to know one important fact. Do not doubt me on this. Remember, I am a leading authority.

You're okay.

Really, you are. All that blabbering, hovering, and interrogation is just a little self-doubt. Your overactive mind and anxious heart just need a little self-esteem recalibration. While I am definitely not an expert on male insecurity or the underlying baggage which causes it, I do know this: you have the power of choice.

I've witnessed too many men who simply choose to stop with the hummingbird act and adopt a healthier perspective of themselves and their lives. They did enough introspection and inner work to allow themselves to experience an epiphany – a BFO (Blinding Flash of the Obvious). It sounds like, "My wife and marriage are not and have never been the source or the measure of my value. I'm okay, dammit. I'm okay!"

When these guys decided to change their operating system, it was like moving their mojo setting from hummingbird to mountain lion. They embraced a whole new demeanor. It's best described as a calm, deliberate, and pleased energy.

It's not an act. They really are mountain lions. They feel cool headed, secure, regal, aware, curious, playful, loving, protective, brave, sensitive, and caring. You may find them on a high rock casually flipping their tail and letting out a huge yawn before taking a nap in the sun.

No more doubts. No more questions. Heart rate: 40 beats per minute.

From that vantage point, anything is possible.

How A Husband Avoided the "Friend Zone" In The Nick Of Time

Being your wife's best friend is fantastic … unless it's the wrong kind of friend.

Bob was nearly crying when he told me something that was really eating at him.

"She told me she feels that we're more like good friends than lovers. We're great parents and we get along perfectly, except she says she really isn't attracted to me "that way" anymore."

I told him he was in the company of thousands of good guys, good dads, and good husbands. What his wife told him is so common it's almost funny … if it wasn't so heartbreaking.

Bob is wicked smart, hardworking, dedicated, loyal, productive, committed, honest, generous, and sensitive. He's focused, dependable and a man of his word. Everyone admires him and appreciates him. Thing is, what he's missing most are the feelings of admiration and appreciation from his wife. He really wants to feel her easy affection and desire.

He wants his lover back.

How Did This Happen?

In Bob's case, this happened a year after their marriage, when he and his wife entered the land of the "ilities."

In her book, *Mating in Captivity*, Esther Perel details the strange but predictable place many couples find themselves after committing to each other. They immediately begin a process of transforming their fun, light-hearted, spontaneous, and flirty pre-marital life into an uptight, restricted, and boring life of responsibility.

Perel lists many other domestic "ilities" like accountability, dependability, respectability, reliability, stability, sensibility, and the worst, predictability. This is the land where bills get paid, retirement plans are funded, kids get fed, the laundry gets folded, and the to-do list gets done. This is the land where two people need to join forces and get shit completed. They grow into a well-oiled team of, well, friends. Friends who get shit done. And they both secretly desire to be a well-oiled team of lovers.

Is This Bob's Fault?

No, it's neither Bob's fault nor his wife's. Stumbling into the land of the "ilities" is one of the most predictable problems couples create for themselves. And they can choose to create something else if they want to.

Finding blame in never part of the solution. But conscious action is. Bob and his wife need to remember what brought them together to start with. None of the words which describe their early energy and attraction ended with "ility." And there is no reason why, starting tomorrow morning, one of them can't begin to reverse the "friend zone" spiral they've created.

Bob told me, "We used to laugh constantly and found the same things hilarious. Then we'd have the deepest, most connected conversations ever. We could be apart for days at a time and not lose a bit of desire for each other. We even had big arguments that always ended with passion."

Perel says this kind of connection and desire is usually the result of erotic energy: mystery, danger, surprise, excitement, spontaneity, separation, unfamiliarity, uncertainty, tension, laughter, and anger. She describes the erotic tension of catching a woman's eye across the room and sharing that knowing, sexy stare that nobody else notices.

What Are You Afraid Of?

Reversing the "friend zone" spiral in a relationship can be scary.

I asked Bob what he feared. Why doesn't he just start being that guy he used to be?

He said, "I'm afraid of looking stupid. I don't know how she will react anymore. I don't want to come across as creepy or needy. Besides, she hasn't initiated any of that, so I don't think she's interested."

"Do you enjoy being the playful, fearless, fun, goofy, sexy guy?" I asked.

"Hell, yes. That was the best time of my life with her!" he said.

"Why were you so comfortable being that guy before you were married?"

"I don't know. I guess I really didn't give a shit what she thought of me, and I didn't have as much to lose."

"So, you initiated erotic behavior all the time and didn't give a shit? You didn't wait for her?"

"Yeah, it was easy, because I knew she liked it and wanted it."

"And what makes you think she's changed?"

Silence.

One Month Later

I received an email from Bob titled "Am I drunk?"

His wife asked him that question even though he stopped drinking a year ago. She commented on how goofy he had been lately, and she wasn't sure what to do with it. At 1:30 in the morning, from her night shift job at the hospital, she sent a one-sentence text to him.

"I love you."

He wanted to know what it meant and how he should view her changing moods. I told him this: When a man decides to simply be the goofy, fun, flirty, sexy man he wants to be, he doesn't need to analyze a woman's moods.

It's quite possible that, at 1:30 in the morning, she was feeling love for the man who wasn't giving a shit what she thought about his goofiness. So, she acted and told him so.

Conscious, deliberate action. Anyone can do it … if they want to.

The Biggest Turn off She Will Never Tell You

Your desperation and low standard for sex is one of the biggest turn-offs for her.

One of the most valuable pieces of information I can share with you about sexual attraction and sexual rejection is this: By the time sexual frustration and conflict enter a relationship, there has been a long road of bad feelings and bad behavior on both sides.

Your wife or girlfriend is crystal clear about the negative energy you both have generated. While she feels bad and emotionally mistreated, she is also keenly aware of how badly she has treated you. In this reality, it is impossible for her to feel sexually attracted to you.

Do you feel the same? Probably not. In fact, most men believe a sexual connection at this point helps to reconnect and smooth over the negativity and erase the bad feelings caused by being treated poorly. She thinks this is insane.

This issue is the biggest turn-off. To her it feels unattractive, un-manly, and a little desperate. She cannot imagine having sex with someone she's not attracted to. Given how horrible she's been and how she treated you, how could you possibly be attracted to her and want sex?

Desperation Is One Of The Biggest Turn Offs For Women

If you consistently make sexual advances toward a woman who feels unattractive she will also find you unattractive. And if you act sexually attracted to a woman who knows she has been acting unattractively toward you, she will lose respect for you.

The old cliché is women need to feel intimacy before having sex while men need to have sex to feel intimacy. Clichés are born for a reason. There's a lot of truth to this. But you're not a slave to it.

So, what do you do? You must choose a new principle for yourself and start operating by it today. The new principle means taking sex off the table unless the feelings you require are present. The new mindset requires you to raise your standards and expectations for her to earn sexual intimacy with you. You are the prize here, not her.

Scary stuff, huh? I know, that is a critical mind-shift.

It's time you hit the reset button and start acting like the prize you were before things got rough. It's time to remember and embrace the beginning you who was irresistible to her before bad feelings and bad behavior became a problem. It's essential to take sex off the table until your conditions are met.

These conditions are first about meeting the expectations you have for yourself regarding how you feel and how you treat her. These conditions are also about her choosing to meet your expectations for how you want to feel and how you expect to be treated. This is called "setting your boundaries," first for yourself, then for her.

Just make the decision to do something different. Something new. Remember …

"Only TWO THINGS change your life: either something new comes into your life, or something new comes out of you."
~Brendon Burchard

Chapter 3
Theory of Operation –
Understanding Your Wife
and What She Needs

> "An unresolved issue will be like a cancer with the potential to spread into other areas of your relationship, eroding the joy, lightness, love and beauty."
> ~JOYCE VISSELL

There are so many things my dad never told me about women and marriage. It would have been so much easier if I had a mentor to teach me the things I explain in the following articles. I've come to understand that each man is ready to learn these things only when he has been banging his head against the wall for a while. My hope is that now is your time. They say when the student is ready his teacher will appear.

Dear Son, Five Secrets I Wish I Knew Before Marriage

This is the letter my dad would have written to his son if he knew what I know now.

I'm a man who is in the business of providing relationship advice for men. I encourage and lead other men to improve their intimate relationships. The path I've taken to this place has been rocky and I've learned things. My clients and I share a history of spending our early years struggling to know ourselves and the women in our lives.

I never received a letter from my dad giving me the "Top Secret" information I would need to succeed in my intimate relationships with women. Most men never do. My rocky ride has since smoothed out. This is mostly due to what I've learned along the way. I don't begrudge my dad for not telling me sooner. He did the best he could do, and I will always appreciate how hard he worked for me.

This is the letter my dad would have written to his son if he knew what I know now.

Dear Son,

As your wedding day approaches I want to give you five things to keep close to your heart in your marriage. I didn't learn these lessons before it was too late for me. Do not make the same mistakes I did!

Before I give them to you, please understand these truths without any self-doubt. Know you are worthy of love. Know you deserve a life of love, inspiration, and passion. Know there will be ups and downs and to expect and embrace them. And know that you always have the power to choose to create good feelings for other people instead of bad ones.

1. She Can FEEL Your Intentions

Your wife has a very special ability to sense negative energy and pressure. She can't "read your mind" but she "feels your love." This "intuition" is widely documented, though many women don't even trust it themselves. But they will react to it. We men are so simple, so direct, so "what you see is what you get." Therefore, we stink at reading between the lines and taking hints.

This is also why we stink at truly understanding the avalanche of emotions we can cause in our women without even knowing it. It's obvious that your angry-toned, table pounding, perfectly logical argument ruffles emotional feathers. What's not obvious is how she feels your intentions. Even without a word, if your energy oozes the least bit of resentment, condescension, or judgment, you have already declared war. And yes, it's your fault. Sorry.

The good news is that your wife feels positive intention the exact same way. Positive intention means positive energy, which means everything you say and do is coming from a different place – a place of love. Instead of judgment, your intention is acceptance. Instead of condescension, your intention is respect. You get the idea. It must be true. You must be authentic. The results you will see in the tone of your conversations are mind-blowing! But you must go first.

I can hear all your "Yeah, but …" arguments now, and I already call "bullshit." There is a way for you to take more ownership for your energy. You can't own her reaction or her happiness, but you can do better, be better – if you WANT to!

2. Don't Ever Think She Is NOT A Sexual Woman

If you ever decide your wife is simply not sexual, not physically affectionate, or ever aroused – you're wrong. Just like you, she is designed for sexual arousal and pleasure. That's about where the similarities end.

She does think about sex. She does have fantasies. She does get aroused. But, if your marriage has tensions, she just doesn't have you in mind.

Don't let life numb your awareness of your responsibility. Sex is not a guaranteed fringe benefit of marriage. It is the result of an age-old cycle of attraction, flirtation, and foreplay. And that's really all she wants. If you lose this recipe she can easily imagine it with someone else. Women simply will not have sex with someone they don't feel attracted to.

The key word to remember is attraction. Without this, flirting and foreplay are a complete waste of time unless you've pushed so hard you wind up with "obligation sex" – the worst possible type! I don't want that for you.

The most important thing to know about attraction is that it will not happen in an environment of bad feelings. You can create feelings of attraction, or not. This ability comes from you knowing who you are, what you believe in, and the direction you go in life. Attracting her to join you means always respecting her and supporting her need to do the same for herself. You are neither superior nor inferior to her. Help her feel that in her heart every day.

While you are not in charge of her moods or behavior, you need to be aware of how you may be involved in her reactions toward you. Becoming attractive to her may involve reversing some damage you unknowingly inflicted. If you have been argumentative, dismissive, resentful, negative, or critical you oversee that and need to get to work.

Why? Because fixing that stuff is important for whatever goals you have in life. If you decide to fix that stuff just to get sex she will know it in an instant! Yes, she really is that good. A man who is willing to resort to "stuff" to earn sex is seen and felt as tremendously non-masculine to a woman.

3. She Has No Choice But To Lead If You're Not Trying

By lead, I mean being the one who chooses to own your part in the marriage and the household. So many men complain about their bossy, nagging, or disrespectful wife. Why? Because they deserve it.

Your wife will rightfully expect and appreciate some leadership from you! Leadership is an important part of the attraction formula. Many men allow their women to lead everything:

- The kid department.
- The laundry department,
- The meal department,
- The cleaning department,
- The relationship department,
- Even the sex department!

It's no wonder these guys find themselves begging for morsels of respect and physical affection. They don't deserve it. You see, the type of leadership I'm talking about is really about your ownership of some of these departments.

Taking responsibility and following through is absolutely sexy. Establishing your personal values for what you're in charge of is sexy. Playing your role in keeping the relationship loving, respectful, and fun is sexy.

This type of leadership finally allows her to feel safe, trusting, and relaxed because you have stepped up. A woman lucky enough to have a man like this doesn't have to resort to nagging or bossing. With the right level of leadership, she will respect you, partner with you, and be proud of you.

4. She Expects You To Understand How To Help Her Emotionally Feel Safe

For both men and woman, emotional safety simply means our emotions are not judged and not subject to debate. It means emotions are respected for being real and important and exactly as they are felt. It means the environment is safe for sharing and discussing our feelings.
Emotions are not supposed to make sense or be logical. Think before you say, "Well, you shouldn't feel that way."

When a woman says, "I hate it every time you lose your temper. It makes me feel, I don't know, I just hate it!" what she's trying to say is, "You have the ability to either make me feel good or bad, and you are choosing to make me feel bad." That choice of yours speaks volumes about your concern and respect for her. It never helps to tell her, "It has nothing to do with you. You shouldn't feel that way." Trust me on that one.

If a man chooses to create an environment of emotional safety, he chooses to understand what behaviors of his can allow that to happen. He chooses to make changes in how he responds to his wife's emotions. He learns the power of a masculine response over a boyish reaction.

5. She Picked You For A Reason

She is attracted to you. She thinks you are funny. She laughs at your jokes. She loves making love to you. She trusts you and respects you. She is proud of you.
Don't screw this up. She loves who you are now. But, you still have a lot of growing to do.

Within the first few years of marriage many men lose sight of the man they want to be and why they chose her in the first place. They can grow impatient, critical, and judgmental. These negative emotions start in very subtle ways during seemingly inconsequential events. If not careful, those events lead to bigger events, and soon men find their wife's trust, respect, and attraction has faded away.

Be the man she married. Be the man she needs. Be the man who is better than trying to "get even" by creating bad feelings in her just because you're feeling bad.

Love her. Give to her without expecting something back. Respect her words and her dreams without judgment.

Talk to her. Be open. Be vulnerable. Let her understand you and your fears. Cry with her.

But don't stop leading! Lead yourself first so you can lead her to a stronger marriage. Accept responsibility. Expect more from yourself. Surround yourself with other good men like you who are on the same path.

I'm one of those men. I'll be with you – for the rest of your life.

Love, **Dad**

10 Ways Your Wife Knows You Don't Think She's Good Enough

Do you play this toxic game? How to change the rules – if you want to.

It's one of the most self-destructive afflictions of the human race – feeling inadequate and not "good enough." Hell, without any help we can manufacture gobs of evidence daily to confirm our own self-doubt. We're quite talented at kicking our own ass without someone else pitching in.

But we choose to bring women into the mix anyway to help finish the job. They are like surgeons when it comes to slicing away our last shred of self-respect. They even know where we store our emergency cache of self-confidence, so they can suck it out of us at will. How did they get this power? How can we defend ourselves?

If you're like a lot of men, you defend against it by returning the favor. With equal and opposite force, you employ your special power to feed her demons of self-doubt and insecurity.

Yeah. Now you're even.

I know this stupid game a little too well after nearly 30 years of practice. I also know how clever we can be at believing we're not playing it.

10 Ways To Confirm Her Feelings Of Inadequacy (Shaming)

In her audio course, *Men, Women and Worthiness,* shame researcher Brene Brown makes a powerful point about people who shame others. She explains that when we shame someone with our criticism, disapproval, or rejection it can usually be tied to a certain shame we feel within ourselves. We hurt in others that which silently hurts in us. She defines shame as "the intense painful feeling or experience of believing we are flawed and therefore unworthy of acceptance and belonging."

If a man feels the pain of inadequacy, unworthiness, and disconnection, he is likely to express that pain in the age-old game of Tit for Tat.

> **Top "Rules" Of The Game For Getting Even***
> - Tell her she doesn't make any sense.
> - Pick at her grammar, writing, or math skills.
> - Frequently express your displeasure about her family.
> - Question her intellectual pedigree.
> - Tell her who you wish she were more like.
> - Try to fix every problem she tells you about for her.
> - Make fun of her friends.
> - Point out her body flaws.
> - Tell her she never wants sex and start ignoring her.
> - Tell her she's always negative and no fun to be around.

*These are gender switchable, but I'm talking to men here.

There are dozens of additional ways couples do this. They rub salt into each other's wounded feelings of disapproval and inadequacy. Then they bemoan the lack of attention, affection, respect, and intimacy. Plus, they are blind to the fact those things cannot possibly exist in the current environment. Each feels hurt and rejected for who they are.

Nothing will change until someone changes.

Hurt People Actually Hurt People

You've probably heard the phrase, "Hurt people hurt people." This basically means a person who has suffered pain at the alleged hands of another is likely to repeat the process.

Given the fact that nearly everyone enters a relationship with some kind of "hurt," it's a dire prediction. Is your relationship just doomed? Is hurting each other something you just have to live with?

I work with men who have been in long cycles of the "Tit for tat, you hurt me I hurt you, I'm not going to change until you change" syndrome. I guess I need an acronym for that.

This is a poisonous process of validating each other's insecurities and feelings of inadequacy. It's a downward spiral of contempt that virtually guarantees misery and divorce. But what if at least one partner chooses to stop playing the game and changes the rules? What if that person decides they want to be unhurt? What's the opposite of unhurt?

What if "Empowered people empower people"?

As Brown points out, "First and foremost, we need to be the adults we want our children to be. We should watch our own gossiping and anger. We should model the kindness we want to see."

How To Change The Rules?

Have you ever seen a football game where the losing team makes an unbelievable comeback? They get their butts kicked in the first half but come back after halftime as a totally different team. It's like they decided to totally change their tactics and mindset. Their

collective mojo is confident, cocky, and amped up. They're on a new

take-charge mission. It's doesn't happen often because it takes focus

and commitment. They have to clearly see the error in the old ways

and want to change

For men playing the "Tit for tat, you hurt me I hurt you, I'm not

going to change until you change" game, it sounds like this:

"This is bullshit. I'm not playing by the old rules anymore. I'm
bringing something totally new to the game no matter what. I'm not
broken and I'm not a loser. I am a better man than the one who
showed up for the first half. I'm not waiting for change. I am the
change, dammit."

Yeah, that sounds a bit like a halftime pep talk, but it's not. Real

transformation is within your grasp if you want it badly enough.

I've seen dozens of men use guilt and discomfort caused by this

toxic game to make a major and permanent shift. It changes their

whole life trajectory in every respect – not just their relationship. It's

a masculine mojo makeover.

It's a decision to not be a victim of circumstance. It's empowerment. A man must choose to lead himself and invite others to join him. It's the choice to be the change you wish to see. I think someone famous said that first.

Three Things She Wants When She Says, "I need you to be the man in this relationship."

If this is what she means by "being the man," is it asking too much?

Hold on tight. This might stir up a hornet's nest, but I don't care. I don't write about how things should be. When a man asks for help I only care about how things are. Then I help him figure out what to think and do next.

When he tells me he just heard, for the tenth time, his wife wants him to "be the man" in the relationship, the last thing he needs to hear is, "Well, dang it all to the hell. It's not the 1950s. She shouldn't be saying stuff like that! You need to discuss equality and the evils of gender essentialism."

And the last thing his wife needs is another discussion about why she shouldn't feel the way she feels.

Let me decode the mystery, or at least part of it, for you. This is what conscious, evolved wives tell me is really going on when they play the "be the man" card.

Why I Have To Tell You This And She Won't

When humans act hurt, frustrated or angry we tend to complain about things in a way that masks our real needs. We may scream in anger at someone who cuts us off in traffic when the truth is we are scared shitless. The real need is that we want to feel safe. But we don't say that.

We may become intensely frustrated with a child when the truth is we are emotionally drained. The real need is that we want to feel peace and calm. But we don't say that.

We may be horribly hurt by something someone says when the truth is we feel rejected. The real need is we want to feel accepted. But we don't say that.

And so it is with many wives. They say things like:

"Why do I have to do everything around here? This place is a disaster!"

"You never follow through, and I can't count on you."

"All you think about is sex."

And the translation husbands hear is, "You suck, you're a bad husband, and you're a pervert."

Dude, that's not what she's saying. I see why you might take it personally, but she doesn't mean to attack your manhood. You have to keep your mojo in check and realize that not every angry woman is angry with you. It's important to know what feeling she craves and why that feeling causes her reaction. It's not about you – it's about her craving to feel something she wants to feel. And she thinks that her "man" could help her feel that if he just knew the three things I'm about to tell you.

"I Just Want To Feel Like I Can Relax."

Wives tell me that feeling relaxed is one of the biggest keys to them also feeling connected, affectionate, and sexy.

Have you ever been around a woman who is being playful, silly, sexy, giggly, fun, and flirty? Yeah, I know. It's about the hottest thing a guy can imagine. It's also an incredibly fun place to be for her. And women tell me they feel like it's biologically impossible to be that girl if she can't relax.

Bottom line: She's mad because she wants to relax so she can feel playful, silly, sexy, giggly, fun, and flirty. She's not mad because you suck. She's mad because she can't relax.

How to "be her man": Don't get defensive. Calmly look her in the eye and say, "Baby, I bet you would love to relax, and I'm going to help with that." Look at the stuff you can help with. Are there plans that haven't been made? She would love you to make a plan – any plan. Be her man with a plan.

What household departments need attention? There are many – cleaning, laundry, kids, cars, vacations, meals, family, dishes, bills, and broken shit. These all require the incredibly boring application of accountability, responsibility, predictability, and dependability. Nobody can relax with all those "ilities!" That means she needs you to be her "ility" man.

Romantic energy gets instantly sucked into the black hole of the "ilities." Don't allow that to happen. Caution: there will be stuff you can't help with. It's her stuff. She needs to handle her stuff, and don't try to handle that stuff for her.

"I Just Want To Feel Like I Can Count On Him."

Wives tell me that when their man is consistent and follows through they feel a sense of safety and predictability. Yeah, those are boring. But with safety and predictability comes relaxation. We've covered the reasons relaxation is so important. See above.

One thing I'm consistent with is her morning coffee. I also like to plan dates and give her invitations to do stuff. I leave notes and call her when I'm going to be late – every time. I like to vacuum – it's like a power tool.

I pick things I expect of myself and I own them. I don't expect or accept her telling me what to own. She knows what I've chosen to expect of myself. She also knows it's her job to pick and own her share of them. This makes for a team effort that helps her feel good and relaxed, which is nice.

Bottom line: She's mad because she wants to feel safety and predictability. You're not a bad husband. She simply can't relax.

How to "be her man": If you want to help her feel like she can count on you, just decide what you expect of yourself. Make it clear what you're in charge of. Then do those things. Consistently.

Less talk. More action

The Stupidly Simple Rule For Men Who Want Better Sex

A simple rule that could turn your sex life around.

I tend to coach and write about the things I most need to heal within myself. And that leads me to the subject of sex. I'm writing this article more for me than for you, but you're welcome to eavesdrop on my internal conversation.

I need to write myself a reminder. A not-so-gentle kick in the ass memo. You see, I've not been taking my own damn advice.

WTF Are You Doing?

If I were to coach myself right now, I would ask, "Steve, WTF are you doing?"

"What? I'm working."

"What would you rather be doing?"

"Umm … I'd rather be swinging in a hammock near a warm beach with a soft, sexy beautiful woman."

"What else?"

"Umm … I'd rather be laughing, teasing, and playing with her while we cuddle, kiss, and taunt each other. Maybe I've got one or two margaritas in me, too."

"What else?"

"Umm … I'd really like to have sex with her. Good sex. Connected sex. Satisfying sex."

"What's one reason you're not doing that right now?"

"Umm … because I'm working?"

"No, it's not just the working. It's your total energy. It's all wrong for getting what you want."

"What do you mean?"

"You're dripping in non-stop predictability, responsibility, accountability, reliability and stability. You haven't looked up long enough to notice the soft, sexy, beautiful woman who lives with you. And when you do you're pretty much faking it."

"Really?"

"Yeah, really. And you've become the poster child for the world's most unsexy man. Your work ethic is admirable, but you're dehydrating every ounce of sexy out of your relationship. You've totally forgotten how to lubricate the erotic side of life. Remember when it wasn't like this?"

"Umm … yeah. I do. I need to fix this."

"Yep. You've forgotten your own stupidly simple rule for creating what you want."

The One Stupidly Simple Rule Men Must Know

I learned this brilliant piece of advice from Esther Perel's *Mating in Captivity*. Every time I have applied this rule in my relationship, everything changed for the better. Being turned on happens in the land of "erotic energy," This is where flirtation, fun, laughter, dancing, danger, and uncertainty live. It's where adventure, surprise, and sensual tension live. And it's where really good sex lives, too. Sure, bathroom floor quickies can happen in the "domestic energy zone." Sometimes they just have to. But the truly satisfying, high quality sex a man really craves will only be found in the "erotic energy zone."

Here's the rule: A man will never encounter deep, connected, satisfying sex in the land of the "ilities." (responsibility, accountability, predictability, etc.) He must consciously and intentionally chart a course and lead the way into the land of the erotic.

Three Simple Steps To Leading Her Into The New Land

There are three simple words to remember: **Connect, Invite, Create.**

The hardest part of doing this is simply making the decision to do it. If you just decide you are going to be the kind of man who forges into the land of the erotic, here is what you must do.

Connect with her by shutting down your domestic mind. This includes shutting off the computer and the phone. Shut down your "work brain." The most important part of connection is your presence. Allow yourself to lean into her world and her energy. Be curious. Be awake. Be aware. Let her know that you really see her, hear her, and understand what her biggest fears and doubts are. **Connect.**

Invite her to join you in the erotic side of life, but you must lead the way. You must go there first. Invite her into a funny moment or a goofy look across the room. Invite her into a spontaneous kitchen dance. Invite her into footsie under the table. Invite her into a dirty joke. Invite her into a five-second kiss. Invite her into a strong, loving hug. Invite her to plan the Caribbean vacation with the hammock and the margaritas. **Invite.**

Create new conversations and new dreams. Paint a picture of what is possible in the new land and how it will feel there. Share a story about two people laughing and flirting in a hammock near the sea while sipping margaritas (note to self). Stop complaining and worrying long enough to compliment and adore her. Inspire her to dream about something bigger than the next load of laundry. **Create.**

Remember: **Connect, invite, create.**

Intimacy and connection only happens when we make it happen. No more excuses. No more waiting for her to initiate. You don't get many second chances to live an erotic life, and this ain't no dress rehearsal.

Chapter 4
THE COLD-STARTING WIFE – HOW TO HANDLE HER COLD, UNRESPONSIVE ATTITUDE

There is nothing more gut-wrenching than the feeling of a woman slowly detaching herself from the love and connection you once knew. The stomach knots of frustration, confusion, and jealousy can tear a man apart. I wrote these articles for men in this position to help them understand some of the dynamics that create the situation. With understanding comes a new perspective. With a new perspective, you can take a new approach from a place of strength instead of fear.

How To Warm Up Your Unaffectionate Wife

Three basic mistakes husbands make in getting the affection they want.

What I'm about to tell you is so mind-numbingly basic you will probably think to yourself, *"Wow, Einstein, is that the best you could come up with?"*

Yep, it's the very best advice I can give to a fellow man, because I know how hard it is to stay focused on the basics. We tend to over-think and over-complicate matters of female love and affection.

If you golf you may remember the times you tried to focus on your feet, your grip, your club, your hips, your knees, your arms, and the wind – all at the same time. Then you shanked it. Ugh.

All you really needed to do was relax, watch the ball, and trust your swing. Just three simple things. Do them consistently and you've got 90% of the game figured out.

It's the same thing when it comes to creating an affectionate relationship. It's not that complicated. The basics matter more than anything else. Your ability to be consistent in the basics is always more important than worrying about where the ball goes (the outcome). As soon as you lose focus on the basics you start slicing every shot.

I'm going to explain three basic mistakes which cause you to "shank it" every time you hope for more affection.

The Difference Between Affection We Get Versus Affection We Give

For the purpose of this article, I define female affection the way my clients describe it:

Female affection to us is any thought, word, or action from her that feels kind, warm, loving, supportive, honoring, approving, accepting, respectful, cuddly, sweet, or sexy. It's the irreplaceable feeling of being wanted and appreciated. It's a feeling of belonging and devotion.

You might say these same things apply to her equally. I'd agree, except for one thing. Most of us devour her affection even if she doesn't really mean it. Even if she doubts her own love and commitment to us. Even if it's half-hearted. Most of us can't tell the difference. And it feels so freaking good that we just don't care.

We want to believe it's true, therefore we do so without question.

But we don't have the same luxury. When we show her affection we

better mean it. Why? We will constantly struggle in our desire for

female affection if we are disingenuous with ours. That gets us

started on number one below.

Three Basic Mistakes That Kill All Wives* Ability To Be Affectionate

* I use the term "All wives" here. By "all," I only mean 99.8%. I apologize to the remaining .2%.

Basic Mistake One: Faking Affection (aka, You Doubt Your Love For Her)

This is so simple it's ridiculous. Don't fake it. It is pointless to

expect any affection at all from a woman for whom your love is in

doubt. Don't play games. This mistake is the number one roadblock

to genuine affection and intimacy. She will not risk giving you

affection if she doesn't trust your love.

Yes, marriage can be full of emotional ups and downs. Doubts

creep in that we must deal with. The rule here is to make sure your

affection genuinely comes from a place of love. Not fear and not

with strings attached. Better to show no affection than to fake it.

If you don't honestly love her and adore her, then you've got bigger problems than an unaffectionate wife. You should be asking yourself different questions. If you are spending time dreaming about your divorce, you're in no place to be bitching about her lack of affection. I know – I tried that once.

Basic Mistake Two: Intellectual Warfare (aka, Trying To Make Her Feel Stupid)

This mistake is also simple but so hard to avoid sometimes. This is the smart guy's tool of choice when the chips are down. It used to be my go-to mode when I wanted to be right about something.

Whenever there is conflict or blame you deftly guide her though a strategic line of logic that leaves her feeling stupid or, at least, feeling like you think she's stupid. The affect is the same. She loses trust.

When you allow your emotions to invoke the intellectual warfare reaction, nothing good happens. Ever. When we allow a conflict to move from a conversation to a court trial the affection factory closes for business.

I won't go into a class on handling conflict effectively right now. Just remember basic rule two. Never try to make her feel stupid.

You're stronger and more secure than that.

Basic Mistake Three: Interrogation (aka, Whiny Questions)

I'm a recovering hummingbird husband, and I've lived this stuff. This is the mistake of asking tons of questions from a place of self-doubt and insecurity. These are questions that have the underlying need of, "Please tell me I'm okay and that we're okay."

They sound like, "What's the matter? Why did you say that? What did I do wrong? What do you want me to do? How can I make you happy?"

To her it feels like a barrage of accusations – an interrogation of her devotion and commitment. When she sees you come from a place of fear, distrust, and doubt, then she can't feel affectionate. I know, a great big hug of reassurance would be the best thing ever. Hell, how about some sex? That would be terrific.

But she can't do it. Why? interrogations make her feel fear, distrust, and doubt. While your fear, distrust, and doubt might be quickly calmed with closeness and affection, hers are calmed mostly by feeling your emotional strength.

Don't ever underestimate the power in your choice to control your reactions and respond from a place of calm, deliberate strength.

Is Your Wife Ice Cold While You're A Hot Mess?

Why your hot mess of vulnerability may be pushing her farther away.

This is bound to tick off idealists who believe "it shouldn't be like that." Sorry. But for scads of married men it is like that.

The cold, hard truth is millions of Openly Vulnerable Husbands (OVH) face cold, distant, and disrespectful wives every day. Even in our "highly-evolved" age there are more questions than answers to the modern marriage and the husbands I help.

Shouldn't This Be A Two-Way Street?

The typical email complaint I get from husbands sounds like this:

My wife and I are really having trouble, and her anger seems to be driving it. She has been calling me needy and hates me talking about my feelings and our relationship. She pulls away when I try to get closer to her and she has been super disconnected. She says she feels smothered by me and my feelings.

I thought we were supposed to show vulnerability to women. I thought we were supposed to be open with them and accept their vulnerability. But she doesn't share anything with me. Shouldn't this be a two-way street?

The answer is no. It's not a two-way street. Let go of what is supposed to be and choose to deal with what is. Your expectation only creates additional cold and more distance.

Wouldn't it be nice if being vulnerable with your wife was easy? Sure, it would. So would financial freedom, effortless sex, and world peace. Like those, it's a lot more complicated than you would like.

The Two-Way Street Myth About Vulnerability

Men and women are perfectly equal – but we're not the same. If sameness is your desire, you need to come back in a new life and give it another shot. Sameness is not going to evolve in your lifetime. Them's the cards you're dealt. You can choose to play or fold.

The two-way street vulnerability myth has a few misconceptions which can leave the OVH quite confused.

1. Men and women should and must display equal amounts of vulnerability in order to create true intimacy, love, and sexual desire.

Expecting to achieve equal amounts of anything is a recipe for disaster. It's easy to manage equity for domestic stuff like housework and bills. But intimacy, love, and desire are not subject to the rules of domestic equality.

Attempts to manipulate equal effort and equal vulnerability is a set up for conflict and disappointment. Pursuing her to join you at a level of vulnerability you desire will cause her to distance herself from you.

2. All women want a man who is willing to show his sensitivity, fears, and tears for her to feel closeness, trust, and sexual attraction.

Even research by vulnerability expert Brene Brown confirms the current social conditioning of women is to be disappointed and disgusted by male vulnerability. Many wives perceive their husband's fear and uncertainty as weakness, and it can scare them, piss them off, and turn them off. One woman explained it to me like this, "I don't mind him being vulnerable, as long as he has a handle on how he is going to fix the problem."

3. It's selfish, unfair, immature, and unevolved for a woman to be turned off by an OVH. She should be the safest place to vent his emotions.

Judging what feels attractive to her is a waste of your time. It's not a conscious choice for her. It's simply a programmed reaction. It's no more selfish, unfair, immature, and unevolved than your reaction to a woman you find extremely unappealing (insert your image here). You could try to rationalize with her that she should be the best, safest place for you to emotionally vomit anytime you feel like it. Or you could try to debate the science of attraction with her to find a resolution. Good luck with that.

A Husband's Job Is To Create Emotional Safety

What emotional safety means to her?

Emotional safety is important to both men and women. Without it we feel unsure about opening up and sharing sensitive emotions and thoughts. Fear of being judged, criticized, or ignored shuts down any hope of communicating at a deeper level on just about any topic. This absolutely affects the ability of two people to connect on an intimate level.

Now, show me a man who has neglected his job in the emotional safety department, and I'll show you a man who has an unhappy marriage and an unsatisfying sex life.

Men always ask me, "Why is this my job?" "Why do I have to go first?" "Why doesn't she have a role in making me feel safe?" The answers have to do with the way we are biologically wired. They have nothing to do with who is stronger, smarter, or more rational.

Your wife or girlfriend is naturally gifted with the ability and intuition to sense your intentions. This means she consciously or subconsciously reacts to your energy and intention. This is her programming and secret power. As a man you do not have this gift. This is why it is your job to behave in ways that create feelings of emotional safety. This is your special gift and secret power.

As your relationship has developed, she has internally cataloged hundreds of emotional data points from you. She can immediately sense what your intentions are when you speak to her or about her, touch her, walk past her, and even when you close a door. It is up to you to understand this and choose to be intentional with your words, tone, and behaviors.

Your words can convey either respect or disdain. Your tone can make her feel loving appreciation or disappointment. Your actions communicate either resentment/anger or calm/self-assuredness. She feels these from you, although she doesn't usually tell you this directly. You must understand the enormous impact your negativity has on her ability to trust you, respect you, and be attracted to you. It is entirely up to you to choose the messages you want to send.

Even if they buy into this, many men say, "Well, I can't be responsible for how she processes her stuff. It's not my fault if she is reacting to me."

Horse hockey. This is like saying you're not responsible for understanding the emotional needs of your child. Or you're not responsible for understanding the mission of your company. Or you're not responsible for the consistency of your golf swing.

If you want to improve your marriage and your intimate life, you have the responsibility for learning what is required. You do not resent the basic fact she needs you to provide emotional safety. In fact, when you become aware of and committed to your masculine role, you find something else is true. The process to become that man is extremely rewarding and fulfilling. It feels like a weight has been lifted from your shoulders when you understand and accept what is needed from you to create emotional safety for her.

This process also opens lines of communication and sharing that you didn't have before. She is able to reciprocate with words and actions that make you feel safer. You finally allow her to feel comfortable in communicating her intimate needs and desires. And you create an environment in which her confident feminine nature will emerge to understand and meet yours.

Chapter 5
TAKING THE DRIVER'S SEAT –
MAKING FAST IMPROVEMENTS BY
IMPROVING YOURSELF

> "Relationships fail because people take their own insecurities and try and twist
> them into their partner's flaws."
> ~STEVE MARABOLI

What if it was true that women reacted to you and not the other way around? What if it was true that you had the power to create a climate where she felt soft, warm, fuzzy, and affectionate any time you wanted? Wouldn't it be great to have such power? Well … you do. You're the "weatherman" in the house, and you can control the climate simply by controlling yourself.

These articles are meant to change the way you think about your personal superpowers. It will astound you how fast things change in your relationship when you decide to be the leader of change.

Relationship Advice From Politicians On What Not To Do

Four bad relationship lessons we can learn from political debate tactics.

Maybe a politician's special gift to humanity is to serve as a bad example. The U.S. presidential debates are like basic training for showing what not to do in your relationship.

Now, in defense of politicians, I must acknowledge they have a very different motivation than you do. Their behavior is driven solely by one critical imperative: They want to be liked. They need to be liked. They hate the idea of not being liked. Yes, they also want to win an election. However, in their list of emotional priorities, I think their desire to be liked and feel significant is at the very top.

What would it look like if a person did this inside their romantic relationship? What if they were more motivated fear of not being liked than they were by the desire to be a good person and partner?

That wouldn't be pretty, would it? They would be acting out of desperation and dependency instead of love and self-confidence. They would see the relationship as a competition. They would do and say a lot of stupid things that would leave them looking silly, smug, superior, condescending, immature and unattractive.

They would look a lot like a politician.

The Perfect Four Point Plan For Acting Like A Politician

1. Be Unaccountable As A Fourth Grader

Refuse to be upfront and honest about yourself until other people do the same. Refuse to acknowledge any weakness or mistake you've made until he/she goes first.

2. Bring up Irrelevant Crap

Distract attention away from yourself by moving the conversation to something totally off point. Pretend you didn't even hear the last thing your partner said so you don't need to address their concern. Pretend you're taking a higher road.

3. Find Blame Instead of Owning Your Shit

Use anything negative you can think about him/her to justify or minimize your own behavior. Blame them for "making you that way."

4. Interrupt Constantly

Dominate the conversation at all times to keep control and give them a chance to make you look stupid. Don't listen because that just gets in the way of you thinking about your next counterpoint.

These four lessons are the perfect plan for anyone who wants to appear insecure, afraid, and about as romantically appealing as a fourth grader. These tactics are born out of a basic unmet childhood need to be liked.

We act like we're in a competition for external approval and validation. We won't give them anything until we feel like we're getting something first. By making them look worse, we might be able to lift our own image, and then we can feel like we're a better person!

Wouldn't it be easier to just actually BE a good person?

How To Be A Good Person And Not Need External Approval and Validation

The first step to becoming a good person who doesn't need external approval and validation is to be clear on who you don't want to be. Watching our politicians is a good place to start. Who else do you know who represents the mindset and behaviors that disgust you? Get a crystal-clear scene in your head of the actors and the script. Understand the actions and the words.

But that's not enough. You can't simply think of what you don't want. That will not drive you toward action and real change.

You have to know deeply and clearly in your heart what kind of person you do want to be. You must have role models to refer to. You must have a vivid picture of the actions and the words you want to embody for you ... and nobody else.

The only way you will ever lose the childhood need of external approval and validation is to learn how to self-approve and self-validate. This happens when you learn to develop a clear sense of who you really are, what values drive you, and where you intend to travel in this life.

When you like who you are when nobody is watching, you won't need them to like you. When your decisions align with your values, you won't need anyone to approve them for you. When you operate from a place of confidence and sense of purpose, you will be a person who has no need to interrupt, blame, or compete with those who challenge you. Your responses come from a calm confidence supported by your values.

You set a high bar for what you expect of yourself no matter what is going on around you. And your future is so compelling that challenges and attacks from others are seen simply as curious opportunities for growth and understanding.

Nothing for a person like you to get rattled about.

Now if we can only get someone like that to run for president.

The Best First Aid for Your Emergency Room Marriage

Some advice for men who feel their marriage is bleeding out.

When men realize their marriage is bleeding out they rush into my "emergency room," which means I receive an urgent email asking for help. I have to remain calm to help them calm down. To breathe and focus.

I also have to help them learn quickly how to not make matters worse. Even with the trauma of "imminent divorce" you must learn how to slow down so you can focus on finding the real source of the bleeding. Panic and thrashing about normally leads to certain death.

Assessing The Urgency Of The Wounds

Triage is vitally important. You don't want to work on wounds that aren't life threatening before addressing the more serious ones. Most guys want to work on everything … all at once.

When I ask about the nature of the injury, I hear a flood of concerns.

"She just isn't responsive anymore."

"She has no pulse for me."

"She says I'm smothering her."

"All she wants is space."

"She says she loves me but doesn't feel "in love" with me."

"We haven't had sex in months."

"She can't tell me exactly where she hurts, so I can't fix anything."

"She says we just don't communicate or connect."

"I think she is having an emotional affair."

I remember being in those shoes. I remember the floundering feeling of not knowing what to say or do next while watching something die right in front of me. I remember trying all kinds of quick fixes.

I remember thinking I should have seen it coming and was now in search of a miracle cure. What I learned is there is no miracle cure. There is nothing you can do to help.

At this point in your marriage the injuries are beyond painkillers and band aids. The best thing to do is simply stop the bleeding. And that requires you to stop doing things that increase the flow.

The Hardest Things You Need to Stop Doing

Guys are doers. When stuff breaks we fix it and move on to the next problem. "There, I fixed it. Next problem."

This doesn't work in an emergency room marriage. In fact, acting like we can quickly patch things up is like rubbing salt into the wounds. It ignores the pain's severity and makes everything worse.

> **How To Stop The Bleeding**
> Pick the ones that apply to you and immediately stop doing them to save the patient.
> - Angry outbursts, yelling, screaming, punching holes in walls, and slamming doors.
> - Questions, questions, and more questions. Heated interrogations.
> - Start any sentence with Who, What, Where, Why, When, or How.
> - Deep, heavy, long conversations until your eyes bleed.
> - Accusations, blaming, finger pointing, and complaining.
> - Ten paragraph texts and emails.
> - Emotional conversations via text message.
> - Texting her every 30 minutes.
> - Sourcing social media sites every five minutes.
> - Snooping, spying, and interviewing friends and family members.
> - Pressuring, pushing, demanding, controlling, and/or dominating the situation.
> - Being nice, super nice, overly nice, or sickening nice.
> - Buying gifts, special dates, vacations, or even a new car.
> - Incessant cleaning and toiling over housework.
> - Crying.
> - Talking about it with your children.

There are many more, but I don't want to overwhelm you. Start with stopping those first and the bleeding will slow down. The more you stop the frantic attempts to fix it, the better chance she may be able to hit the reset button.

Patience at this time is excruciating, and there's no guarantee she will change anytime soon, if at all.

I know, it's like being crushed by your own car and having the paramedic say, "Sir, I need you to stay calm." You know he's probably right, but he doesn't have a freaking car sitting on his chest.

You need to breathe, get a grip, and stay focused.

The Best Thing You Can Do Isn't "Doing," It's "Being"

This is not going to be easy. You're either going to have to take a leap of faith that I know what I'm talking about or basically go ahead with your plan.

The best gift you can give to yourself and her right now is a consistent energy of calm confidence. You don't need to physically do anything. All you need to be is unshaken, cool-headed, and compassionate.

You need to be focused on how you think about this. No matter what she says, this situation is not all your fault. You're not a mean, horrible man, or an inadequate husband. Her downward spiral must not suck you down with it. You can't help yourself or anyone else if you go down there.

Down there … that's where guys do those 16 things listed above. The best way to avoid the downward spiral is to know one absolute truth – you've got a higher purpose right now.

This is not the time to lose your shit. You owe it to yourself and your family to stay clear-headed and strong. This is not all about you, and you can't allow it to crush your soul.

Is part of it about you? Yes, no doubt. And this is the time when men can use this realization to spark a major mojo transformation or whip themselves up into a hot mess that lasts for months or years.

When you understand the real reasons many women spin out of control and away from their relationships you won't feel so personally attacked. This allows your pulse and respiration to drop and makes it possible for you to have empathy for some of the confusion and pain she is going through.

Yeah, empathy. This is part of your mojo transformation that changes all your relationships – maybe even this one. When you can muster true empathy, you can stop doing those destructive things and start feeling your own clear, calm, confident strength within.

From my experience this is often the only thing she really needs

from you at this very moment.

Chapter 6

BACKING OFF THE GAS – HOW TO BUILD ATTRACTION BY DOING LESS

> "No one is in control of your happiness but you; therefore, you have the power to change anything about yourself or your life that you want to change."
> ~BARBARA DEANGELIS

I often tell men there's no such thing as "saving a marriage." A marriage is simply the resulting energy of how two people choose to show up with each other A struggling marriage doesn't need to be saved – only the two people involved, and you've got 100% control over half of that.

These articles were written to give you a solid understanding of why "saving yourself" first has the best chance of improving your relationship. I want you to feel clear and strong about your ability to inspire and invite your partner to join you at a higher level of relationship. But you must learn how to go there first – with or without her.

Dear Spouse: I Can't Get Close Until You Back Off

She chases. He retreats. This pattern destroys marriages.

Jane: "Why do you always do that?"
John: "Do what?"
Jane: "You ignore me. Everything is more important to you than me."
John: "No, it's not."
Jane: "We need to talk about this. You're doing it now."
John: "I don't see the problem. You're overreacting."
Jane: "No, I'm not!"
John: "I don't want to talk about this anymore."

Jane is pursuing. John is distancing.

In her study of 1,400 divorced individuals over 30 years, divorce expert E. Mavis Hetherington found that couples who were stuck in this mode were at the highest risk for divorce. Researcher Dr. John Gottman of the University of Washington and The Gottman Institute also noted this destructive pattern is common cause of divorce.

He claims that, if left unresolved, the pursuer-distancer pattern continues into a second marriage or subsequent intimate relationships.

What Is It Exactly?

Therapist and author Dr. Harriet Lerner (https://www.harrietlerner.com/) summarizes the pattern like this:

"A partner with pursuing behavior tends to respond to relationship stress by moving toward the other. They seek communication, discussion, togetherness, and expression. They are urgent in their efforts to fix what they think is wrong. They are anxious about the distance their partner has created and take it personally. They criticize their partner for being emotionally unavailable. They believe they have superior values. If they fail to connect, they will collapse into a cold, detached state. They are labeled needy, demanding, and nagging.

"A partner with distancing behavior tends to respond to relationship stress by moving away from the other. They want physical and emotional distance. They have difficulty with vulnerability. They respond to their anxiety by retreating into other activities to distract themselves. They see themselves as private and self-reliant. They are most approachable when they don't feel pressured, pushed, or pursued. They are labeled unavailable, withholding, and shut down."

Lerner points out the importance of recognizing that neither pattern is wrong. In a normal relationship, we may actually take turns adopting one role or the other. Healthy relationships can handle the stress with mutual respect and appreciation.

Both partners are aware of their behavior and are willing to adjust it for the benefit of the relationship.

The problem that most commonly leads to the dismantling of the marriage is when partners become entrenched in the roles. If something does not change, both begin to feel criticized and develop contempt for each other—two of the major warning signs that their marriage is doomed to fail, according to Gottman.

What Does It Look Like?

A common scenario: a wife is very anxious over the lack of communication from her husband. She wants him to open up to her more. She wants him to be more vulnerable and to connect with her so they can work on getting along better. His response is, "I don't know what you're talking about."

She pushes harder, and he moves away. Her frustration shows as she begins to criticize him, and he returns the volley. She becomes angry, and he builds an emotional wall of isolation. She can't imagine why he won't see how wrong and stubborn he is. He can't believe she doesn't know how unfair and brutal her pressure feels to him.

Gottman believes the tendency of men to withdraw and women to pursue is wired into our physiology and reflects a basic gender difference.

I'm not so sure about that. I've seen so many examples where the roles were reversed that it appears pursuing or distancing is more about personality than gender.

I've coached dozens of men who were the full-time pursuers. They pursued sex, emotional connection, affection, communication, appreciation, attention, and respect. Their debate tactics were legendary. They crafted incredibly impassioned and rational arguments which proved beyond a doubt that she was wrong.

All she needed to do was agree and get with the program. They didn't stop until they got agreement. They learned that never happens.

Both men and women can be pretty good pursuers. I think the skill is best used for pursuing mutual happiness rather than our own righteousness.

Why Does It Matter?

I have no reason to debate Gottman's theory on gender-based pursuer-distancer patterns. The research by Gottman and

Hetherington is important. It can save marriages or save an individual from a life of bad relationships.

The research sheds light on the extremely common dynamics that happen in everyday relationships with everyday people. It gives language and insight to the thoughts, emotions, and behaviors which consistently cause the end of relationships. The relative statistics don't matter as much as what a person chooses to do with the information.

That's all that ever matters when it comes to our relationships. What conscious choices do we make? What do we expect of ourselves in our thoughts, emotions, and behaviors to increase the likelihood of a happy, respectful, and enduring relationship?

With proper information and willingness, human beings can choose how they respond to relationship stress and intentionally diffuse criticism and contempt. They can be less aggressive pursuers and more engaged distancers if they want to be.

Pursuers Must Go First

Lerner notes something I see consistently with male clients who are pursuers.

"The pursuer is the one in more distress about the distance, and more motivated to change the pattern. For this reason, the pursuer is often best served by discovering ways to call off the pursuit—and there are ways to reconnect with a distancing partner that don't involve aggressive pursuing. A distancer may feel unhappy about how things are going in a relationship, but he or she is still more likely to maintain the status quo than to move toward a partner who is in pursuit mode."

This is the reality faced by the pursuer men I work with. Their distancer-partners' abilities to maintain the status quo are mind boggling. They stay in distancer mode for years while he keeps trying the same old tactics. They feel powerless to move toward him because they need first to feel a release of the intense pressure of the men's relentless pursuits.

The impact on a woman's ability to trust after years of pursuit can be enormous. It's hard for him to understand her fear and skepticism about reconnecting. Rebuilding trust requires a consistent and dependable energy of acceptance and respect. She wants to feel less pressure, less judgment, and less anger.

When he chooses to understand and empathize with her critical needs, he can choose a new mindset. He can consciously draw back to focus on other things. He can love her in ways that pull in instead of pushing her away.

He can choose to learn what that means for her.

What if she is the pursuer? Everything applies the same. She has the same responsibility.

Distancers Beware

Lerner also gives a warning to distancers.

"But distancers beware: Many partners, exhausted by years of pursuing and feeling unheard, leave a relationship or marriage suddenly. When a distancer realizes that a partner may actually walk out, he or she may flip into a position of intense pursuit. But it may be too late."

What Does This Mean For A Distancer?

She must realize the power she holds in how she chooses to respond to his desire for connection. A choice to create feelings of fear and inadequacy in her partner also sabotages her own chance for a rewarding relationship.

She must be aware of what she is avoiding and why. Just because her partner is pressuring her doesn't make him wrong. Maybe his expectations are reasonable and she resists feeling controlled.

Maybe he is calling her out on something she knows darn well could be improved, but she resents him pointing it out. She must be honest with herself.

And if he is truly being unreasonable and unfair, then she should step right into his space and calmly tell him so without hesitation. She should firmly stand her ground from a place of love and respect.

The worst thing for a pursuer to feel is detachment. When they are given the gift of genuine presence and attention they are able to relax and back off so much easier – even if you disagree.

Of course, a man who is distances has the same responsibility.

Starting All By Yourself

Must both people do their work at the same time in order to escape the pattern? No, and expecting it to happen will negatively affect their ability to start making their own changes.

The changes must be driven by a desire to be a better partner—not to get some instant result or reciprocation. Pursuers are known for being outcome dependent and have a hard time making changes without expectations. Distancers are known for being stubborn and have difficulty making the first move when under pressure.

When one person makes a commitment to change their approach and their responses on a consistent basis, their relationship changes. The first change is you feeling better about yourself.

The second change is normally your partner feeling good about you feeling good.

This is a really strong start. It can only get better from there.

How To Stop Trying To Make Her Happy And Still Get What You Want

Why the myth of "Happy Wife – Happy Life" may be ruining your relationship.

I get to collect a lot of data from frustrated married men. These are the guys who "never communicate their thoughts and feelings." Actually, they do. The floodgates open when they are in a place of safety and trust. Unfortunately, their marriage is missing both. So, they share their deepest secrets with me, and I've memorized their painful comments.

Have You Said Any Of These Things?

- I feel her anger on a daily basis.
- She has no respect for me, and she always finds fault in what I'm doing.
- I feel unimportant, and I'm her lowest priority.
- A kiss goodbye in the morning is a major effort for her.
- She has no interest in my affection, and our sex life is non-existent.
- Every time I try to do something to make her happy or connect with her I'm met with sarcasm or disapproval.
- I'm almost done with this.
- I want a marriage that is happier, more respectful, and more intimate.

It's Not About What You're DOING. It's About Who You're BEING

Have you grown up believing that respect, connection, and intimacy are automatic benefits of doing things to make women happy? While this mode of operation can make your boss happy, it is useless in your romantic relationship. It's worse than useless. It's destructive, and it only gets worse the harder you try.

By continuing to operate in a "Make Her Happy" mode you create an environment of bargaining and entitlement. It's an implied contract you've created all by yourself. To her it feels like you're thinking, "If I keep doing this, she will owe me that." This mode can very well earn you a raise at work, but it will make the woman in your life run for the hills.

To you it may feel like disrespect, distancing, and rejection. That is not intentional on her part. She is simply reacting to a bad deal just like you would to a sleazy salesman at a used car lot. You will likely take her reaction personally, and this will make matters worse as you spiral down into the incredibly unsexy territory of resentment, blame, and contempt.

I used to be the ambassador for that territory. It's not something I'm proud of. They were dark days, and I couldn't leave until I learned a whole new lesson about how I was being.

We Teach Men More About What To DO Than How To BE

My pre-marriage education on how to be a man was full of "What to Do's." These came from male role models who were my only teachers.

The What To Dos

- Get a job and pay the bills.
- Fix stuff around the house.
- Be nice and apologize when she's mad.
- Help with the chores.
- Compliment her.
- Allow her to make all the plans.
- Remember anniversaries
- Say, "Yes, dear" when needed and don't rock the boat.
- Compromise. Negotiate. Sacrifice.

It was never actually stated, but my teachers implied that doing those things was key to a man's happiness. I trusted that, if I did these things, then I could expect a respectful, connected, and intimate marriage – just like theirs.

There was one problem I didn't see until much later. None of my teachers actually had a marriage like that. They blindly passed down the same "wisdom" they were handed decades earlier. I didn't pay much attention to the unhealthy lack of respect, connection, and intimacy in their relationships. It was my "normal," and it became my fate.

I became a husband who settled for the same mediocre results my teachers settled for, and I attracted a partner whose teachers taught her to do the same thing. With each passing year we kept doing the same things as we gradually lowered our expectations for ever having the relationship we really wanted.

At the inevitable end of my 28-year marriage, I started my journey in learning how to stop doing things to get things. It was time to learn how to be a man who gets what he wants.

How to Become A Man Who Gets What He Wants

This change requires you to retool yourself and your mindset. What you do now is probably not getting you what you want. You must acquire new knowledge, new skills, and a new perspective to become a man who gets what he wants by being different than you have been. You must be more focused on the process of becoming a man who gets what he wants than you are on getting the outcomes you desire.

Respect, trust, and connection are created by holding the values of respect, trust, and connection rather than chalking up brownie points to "win" those things. When you live in accordance with these values you become a man with no expectations that others must change to please you. You learn your value is not defined by the approval or happiness of your partner. You operate in a mode where you are already pleased with yourself.

This is the key difference between men who have what they want and those who don't. They are willing to change who they are BEING in order to be pleased with themselves – not to please others or gain their approval.

They become clearly aligned with the expectations they have of themselves and for themselves. By seeing their own value, they confidently invite others to join them in the life they plan to have. They want their partners to share respect, trust, and connection with them. Yet, they don't need them to.

They are so clear and confident about their own value that pouting, arguing, and complaining are no longer options for them. Those options disgust them.

Their sense of well-being is not found in women agreeing with them, liking them, or having sex with them. They are secure in themselves. They are certain they will have the life they want. And they know they can't control their partner's choice to join them. A feeling of liberation replaces self-doubt.

Patience, Process And Faith

It's helpful to know why some men fail and never become someone who gets what he wants. There are three reasons that show up in most men I know:

1. He's impatient and overly invested in outcomes.
2. He fails to understand and accept the process is totally within his control.
3. He doesn't believe what he's deserving and capable of creating what he wants.

It's amazing how quickly you start to see changes when you consistently apply patience, process, and faith to the changes you make. But your focus must be on yourself, not expected outcomes. Men who focus on outcomes are impatient for results, and they start doing things all over again to force what they want. This blows up in their face every time and sets back the whole process.

A recent client said it perfectly in an email:

"I am so happy that throughout this entire process I was able to get to a place where the outcome of my relationship status became secondary to simply putting in the tough work to become a better man. Period. And yes, you can use that quote." ~ John K.

Patiently create change with a process of inward focus without forcing expectations on others and anger and blame start to fade away for you. Accept your ownership of the process and your power to hold yourself accountable to a new set of values. Confidence and optimism begin to wash over you. Believe that this is the man you're supposed to be and can create whatever you want. A door will open and a light will come on.

I call this your epiphany.

Start Creating The Relationship And Life You Want

There is a brutal truth all men must face. Nothing will change in your relationship or life unless something changes within you. Of course, there is the possibility that someone else may make changes for you.

It's better to be proactive here. You will make a difference immediately in your relationship if you stop doing things out of expectation. Decide to be in charge of your own mindset, attitude, and responses. Take ownership of those things because it's who you are, not for what it will get you.

Set new expectations for yourself and how you will operate no matter what. Consistently be more respectful, trusting, and connected with everyone around you … especially your partner. Don't make the same mistakes that others make. Make patience, accountability, and faith your new best friends.

You can have the relationship and life you want if you simply decide you want it, own it, and deserve it.

If all this sounds challenging … it is. Getting what you want requires a little elbow grease. It can feel a little messy and a little scary. Fear can make a man stay stuck.

I want you to feel your mojo again. There is no better feeling for me than watching a man get unstuck and creating the life he wants.

How To Improve Your Marriage By Caring Less

Some straightforward advice for husbands who care too much about things they can't control.

I work with a lot of men who I can relate to. They are results driven men. Fast thinkers. Good talkers. Articulate, insightful, and opinionated. Mix that stuff with a heavy dose of being emotionally intuitive, sensitive, hopelessly romantic, and sexually "amped up" – well, we're pretty much screwed.

Sometimes we don't know when to shut up and not argue. We have a hard time just chilling out and leaving well enough alone. It's like a dog that springs off the freaking deck every 10 minutes to bark at the next round of nothing whatsoever (I'm looking at that little bastard now, which is where the analogy came from).

We're not remotely aware how our energy can feel to those around us like a woodpecker trying to knock a hole through a steel gutter at five in the morning (That was yesterday). We notice everything, feel everything, and we try to control the outcome of every interaction. But we know something isn't right. Feeling like a nervous, anxious hummingbird husband isn't how it's supposed to be.

In other words, we care too much. As Mark Manson said in his epic article (www.markmanson.net), we can give way too much of a f*ck about things we shouldn't. We need to ration our f*cks.

We must protect our f*cks and use them much more wisely. If you can relate to this, I am suggesting it's time to care much more about your own mojo and much less about your marriage.

First things first – this is the key to your future happiness, in every respect.

I like the way a client said it a while back.

"It's so freaking liberating to not care so much about every little thing that's out of my control. I can finally relax … and so can she."

Why We Tend To Care So Much

In my case, and with every man I work with, it all starts with a story in our head. It's a story about how things are supposed to go. How the marriage is supposed to feel. What she should be doing to make us feel better. The story is hard-wired with very specific details about how our whole life is supposed to be and how this relationship is supposed to serve us. Our significance in this world and our value as a man and husband are tied directly to this story coming out right.

This creates a huge set of expectations over which we have no control. And when things go off track, we get nervous, insecure, anxious, angry, uptight, worried, and controlling. The story isn't happening like the script said it would. Then we say things that make matters worse and we do things we regret.

If only everybody else would fall in line with the script, dammit, everything would be fine!

The Problem With The Script

The problem with the script is that it's missing a key part. The leading man never written in his version. He doesn't actually know a thing about his role. He only knows what the supporting cast is supposed to be doing. The story of who he is, his beliefs, and expectations of himself aren't fleshed out yet.

The author didn't develop his character and his motivations. He doesn't know his own lines, responsibilities, or boundaries.

Therefore, he must improvise. He must make it up as he goes – reacting to everything –knowing that one way or another, he is supposed to end up happily ever after. This sucks because he's a really bad actor and everyone knows it. Down deep he knows it, too. All of his feelings and reactions are bubbling out of place of fear and uncertainty.

Finding his authentic center is going to mean finding himself and defining his role in this story. Without this, all he can do is care about everything and everyone except for who he is. This is the place in a man's life where his reactions, feelings, and decisions come from a place of fear and uncertainty. It's the most accurate predictor of how the next 30 years of his life are going to go.

The reason he's afraid to change anything about himself now is because he's afraid he'll lose what already created. But his grip on that is loosening every day and he knows it. So, he's torn between deciding to make drastic changes in himself and waiting to see what changes are going to happen to him.

I always recommend writing your own next chapter.

Chapter 7

KING OF THE ROAD – HOW TO OWN

YOUR ROLE AND BE A LEADER SHE

RESPECTS

> "A leader is one who knows the way, goes the way and shows the way."
> ~JOHN C. MAXWELL

"Lead" has become a four-letter word in today's politically correct environment. People incorrectly assume there's imbalance of power if someone tries to lead. They imagine a controlling, domineering style, and they bristle at the idea of being led by another.

I wrote these articles to clarify what leadership is all about in your relationship. It's more about how you lead yourself and your energy in order to lead the energy of the relationship. If you don't know how to lead, then she will have no choice but to take all the responsibility. And that never works out – as you may already know too well.

The Man You Need To Be To Have The Relationship You Want

You can either go big or go home. Which one do you choose?

I get to hear a lot of stories about men and marriage counseling—most not very good. This is because a lot of men kind of suck at the counseling process. They are way too passive and simply follow the lead of the counselor and their wife. They actually believe the best solution is to passively become a cog in the wheel of a healing process created by someone else. They simply show up with no agenda other than to cooperate and not make anyone madder than they already are.

Here's the truth: Nothing destroys your masculine confidence and optimism more than when you leave your leadership role to someone else. When men contact me looking for help it's usually right around this time. They're done with wishy-washy. No more walking on eggshells. It's time to go big or go home.

That's exactly what Brian did for months. He was mad at himself for how he had been showing up. He decided it was time for a change. It was time to take the lead – no matter what happened next.

It Was Time For Real Feelings And Real Truth

Brian told me he was sick and tired of the "wheel spinning" going on in his counseling sessions. The exercises started out interesting, but he and his wife, Marcy, always ended up back in the same spot.

Later Next Week

Brian sent me an email after his counseling session was over to let me know how things went. His message was brief.

"Hey. It was awesome. I felt so clear. I was just me – the way I want to be. I was on the edge of the couch and more engaged than ever before. When the time was right I just spit it out. It was authentic. I felt strong. For the first time ever the counselor was speechless. He looked kind of shocked. He looked at Marcy and she just stared at me – no words. I actually felt bad for her and just wanted to hug her. We're home now. All she has said since counseling, "Wow. Where has that guy been for the last ten years?" I know what she means and it sucks. But I'm okay and plan to stay strong. I have no regrets for what I said. I guess we'll find out how this all turns out before long. But, man, this sucks. I love this woman. Thanks."

There is no such thing as "saving" it. You can only create new stuff from this point forward. You can only speak your truth. Be crystal clear about what you want and what you expect of yourself.

You can only hold yourself accountable to the mindset and the non-negotiable values that will drive you as a man each day. Show up like this every day – everywhere – even in counseling sessions.

It is this guy who gets to create the life and relationships he wants. It is only this guy who stands a chance of reinventing his marriage.

All you can do is invite others to join you on your journey and lose all attachment to their choices. You do this by learning stuff nobody ever told you about the power of masculine confidence, clarity, and optimism! You will be good either way. That's the whole point. When you do this work, you discover that your happiness is guaranteed no matter what other people choose to do with their lives.

Will there be sadness? Yes. Lots of it. There will be lots of joy, too.

Both are needed to keep your journey authentic, assuming that's what you want.

Who Is Leading Who In Your Marriage?

The most important leadership skill in your marriage may not be what you think.

Dad should be the leader of the family.

No, wait.

If Mom ain't happy, ain't nobody happy.

No, wait.

Men need to be the King and treat their wives like Queens.

But, if you treat her like a Queen, she'll think of you as her King.

Clichés and metaphors are cute but can cause a lot of confusion.

Shouldn't there be a clear answer?

Maybe It's More Like A Flock of Geese

Everyone knows the story of how geese fly together. Maybe not.

They fly in a "V" shape and play a combination game of leapfrog and follow the leader. They each take a turn as the lead goose in the "V," which is the hardest position to play.

That goose is the only one breaking wind, so he/she gets tired a lot more quickly. The others get to draft behind someone else to conserve energy for their turn at the leader spot. They keep switching around so everyone gets a chance to rest – a chance to follow.

Pretty cool arrangement. I wonder who thought that one up.

What If Couples Operated The Same Way?

They would glide through their relationship with ease, and it would also be hard to tell who the leader is. They would have this cool arrangement where they both get to lead and follow at the same time. It would look effortless to outsiders who couldn't discern the rules of the game they played.

There would have to be an inherent appreciation and respect for each other's leadership skills and willingness to follow. They would have to want to go in the same direction and under the same set of rules. They would have to share the same love of the game and the values that define it.

Have you ever seen a couple like that? It seems to me the only way that could happen is if each person were less concerned about leading the other and more focused on leading themselves.

Therefore, each partner is a very important leader – at all times.

That reminds me of another cliché: you must become the partner you wish your partner to be.

Hmm ... that sounds a little like leadership, too.

What Does Leading Yourself Mean?

This is the hard part.

Now that the fairytale part of my article is over, the questions become:

"How do I do that?"

"How do I become a better partner when she is cold and he is such an ass?"

"How do I lead her when she doesn't even respect me"

"How do I lead him when he doesn't even listen to me?"

Leading yourself to become a better partner – one who deserves a great partner – requires an incredibly selfish mindset. This is about you. Only you. Nobody else but you. This is where you figure how to love and care for yourself first so you can be strong enough to love and care for someone else. Leading yourself means learning how to give her/him something to follow.

You can't give a rat's ass (another good cliché) about what she/he chooses. You can't give a crap what she/he thinks about you and your values. You can't be focused on what she/he isn't doing because you will never be able to see what you need to be doing for you.

And if you can't see what you need to be doing, you will react to everything. You will mirror negative energy. You will find yourself arguing, complaining, and nagging over stupid things. You will end up negotiating, sacrificing, and compromising the very values you know can lead to an amazing relationship.

Leading yourself means you're very, very clear on where you're going. It also means knowing when to not follow someone who isn't capable of going where you're going. In the end, if you don't know where you're going, then you'll be easily led anywhere and wonder how you got there.

That may be a cliché someday.

What A Horse Can Teach You About Your Wife: Lessons From A Horse Whisperer

If you can communicate with a horse, you can communicate with your wife.

In my work with married men struggling with their relationship I use any tool I need to make a breakthrough. Sometimes, my background in horse training comes in handy to create ah-ha moments for my frustrated clients.

Understanding how horses think and feel while trying to communicate with them is not an easy task. That's why horses are so commonly used to teach trust, leadership, respect, and empathy in dozens of ways. Just search Horse Therapy on the internet to find out how traumatized and disabled people, disadvantaged kids, and even corporate managers develop communication and empathy skills through horses.

It can be very beneficial personally for men to learn about the bond that lures thousands of young girls and older women into the horse's web of seduction. A woman's ability to empathize with a horse's vulnerability and acute awareness of how pressure is felt seems to come naturally to them.

If a man wants to begin actively and purposely to improve his relationship with his lady, there' a lot he can learn from the horse's secrets. Learning to communicate his intentions in the language that feels right to her can begin to unwind years of misunderstandings and feelings of disrespect and disapproval. In other words, he can learn to empathize with his wife.

Lack of empathy is one of the most common complaints I hear from unhappy wives. If you can grasp the skills of communicating effectively with a horse, you can begin to understand your wife's perspective and experience of trying to communicate with you.

A True Story At Every Ranch – Every Day

There's a ranch hand working with a three-year-old horse in a round pen. The horse is new to the ranch and, in its short life, has learned to fear and distrust people.

The ranch hand is being watched by the head horse trainer who has developed a reputation as one of those "natural horsemen" or "Whisperers."

This is the seventh day in a row the young man has found himself with this horse in this pen for two hours trying to do one thing. All he wants is the horse to trust him enough to quit running in circles, snorting, sneering, and kicking at him. Well, he also wants the horse to walk into the middle of the pen and stand quietly with him.

And he wants her to believe he won't hurt her – that she is safe with him – that she will "join up" with him as calm, trusting horses are able to do. He wants to touch her without her getting wide-eyed and backing away. Furthermore, sometime soon, he wants to ride her and have her be okay with it – even enjoy it.

The Whisperer watches the young man mumble cuss words at the horse, swing his rope, wave his hat, and glare at her eyes as he chases her in circles. *Stupid horse*, the ranch hand thinks to himself.

The head trainer finally speaks.

Sometimes A Guy Doesn't Know What He Doesn't Know

"What am I doing wrong?!" the young man asks.

"Well," the trainer starts, "it'll take another seven days to answer that question, so I won't try. You'll be better off knowing what that mare needs from you to trust you. I thought you might start to get it after a while, but it's not uncommon to see guys just try the same old stuff with more gusto thinking she'll come around."

Putting a hand on the young man's shoulder, he says, "Over the last few days I've watched how you are with her. You're loud. You're bossy. You act unsure of yourself. You yank on her halter. You wave your arms a lot. You act scared of her. She thinks you're scared of her."

He continues. "Let me explain what she needs and why. Knowing this will help you choose how to act better tomorrow. First and foremost, she needs to feel your respect. This is not the same as you saying you respect her. She will know based on how you act.

"She can't feel respect from you when you are unaware of how she receives your attempts to communicate. The horse is not a mind reader, but she can feel the pressure of your intentions – good or bad. Everything you've communicated to her this week felt like control, disappointment, frustration, and demands. Your uncertainty with her reactions to you felt like distrust and fear. And the negative energy of your foul grumbling felt like disapproval. You say you want her to stand next to you, but she feels your urgency to get a saddle on her and ride. She is having a hard time just relaxing and being a horse in your presence."

What's REALLY Going On Here?

A horse's ability to trust, touch, respect and enjoy the company of a person comes with conditions. With an ability to feel the smallest fly land on their butt, they feel the intention and pressure from everything around them. They need to feel a calm confidence from people. They enjoy the predictability of an even-temper and purposeful assertiveness. They are literally attracted toward a person, or another horse, who creates feelings of safety, relaxation, and fun.

Yep. Horses like fun.

They prefer to be "asked" or "invited" to do things for people with the smallest amount of pressure. Horses hate excessive pressure. Although they begrudgingly respond to it, they always prefer the presence of the horse or person who can make them feel accepted and safe with the least amount of pressure.

Horses become restless with excessive eye contact, an aggressive approach, and overly tentative behavior.

Oftentimes, the very best "release of pressure" to a horse is to simply back off. Give her space. Allow her the freedom she was born with. A lot of people crowd horses with touching, affection, and constant attention. It freaks them out.

They need time away from the expectations of being perfect. This time and space allows them to reconnect with people more readily and willingly. The person who can achieve this with a horse is able to form the partnership they seek. Some of the most amazing, mutually respectful relationships I've seen are between a person and a horse who seem to delight in doings things for each other just for the fun it.

What's In It For You?

It's funny. Men who learn to work effectively with horses never question "what's in it for them?" When they learn what's really going on, it's obvious why they need to be the one to initiate a better environment for the horse. However, men who struggle in their marriages are not so quick to understand, and I get it.

Like their wives, these men have also been experiencing some very real pain, disrespect, and distrust in their marriage. The decision to accept part of the responsibility for that reality is a tough one. But just like the young man in the story, continuing to operate the same way every day always yields the same results. I encourage and lead men to choose a new way of operating – first for their own good, then for their marriage.

In my personal experience, the process of learning this uncovered some vulnerabilities of my own that hid under "cow pies" for decades. I discovered a language that has helped me to be honest with myself and to better express my feelings with the woman in my life. If thinking of horses helps me understand what she needs, I'd like her to think of me as a Labrador Retriever. A few belly rubs and one, "You're such a good boy!" keeps me feeling safe and desired all day long.

Chapter 8
Sexy Ride – Getting
Perspective on Sex and
Romance

> "What counts in making a happy marriage is not so much how compatible you are but how you deal with incompatibility."
> ~LEO TOLSTOY

Let's be honest with each other. You are a sexual being. You like sex. You think about it all the time. You got married with an expectation that sex was part of the bargain. But you're finding out that it's not a simple fringe benefit. It just doesn't happen on its own, does it?

This chapter is meant to give you a glimpse into the inner game of sex and intimacy. Men who have satisfying sex lives have figured this out. They have mastered their sexual energy and the outward expression of their desire. You can learn how to create trust, emotional safety, and positive sexual tension with any woman. This is what your wife wants most from you.

Is Sex So Important That You Would Leave Me And Our Kids?

Have you ever had this conversation? It's not really about the sex ... is it?

Bill and Sarah were at it again. Over the last 15 years it seemed this conversation had no end. Nevertheless, that didn't stop Bill from trying.

Bill: We can't just keep going on like this!

Sarah: Like what?

Bill: Once again you're not in the mood for sex and I get rejected. I want to talk about it and you don't. We never reach any resolution to this. And your indifference is pissing me off.

Sarah: I'm not indifferent. It's just not the only thing I think about like it is for you.

Bill: It's not all I think about, but it's important to me to have an intimate connection with my wife.

Sarah: Oh, whenever you want to have sex you call it an "intimate connection," so I appear to be the cold-hearted witch. This is why I don't want to talk about it. You make me feel horrible when we talk about it.

Bill: All I'm saying is that a healthy sex life is normal, and we're not normal, and I don't know how much longer I can deal with it. I can't see me doing this for another 15 years.

Sarah: There's a lot of other stuff in our marriage that isn't normal either, you know.

Bill: Like what?

Sarah: Like the way you treat me, talk to me, and criticize me. Is sex so important to you that you would leave me and our kids?!

Bill: No, yes, I mean I don't know … Aargh! … What kind of question is that? Who said anything about leaving?

This is the same conversation Bill and Sarah have about every six months. It's always the same. Bill tries his same logical approach to solve the sex problem, and Sarah ends the conversation by challenging his dedication to his family. It sounds like they aren't even close to being on the same page in this discussion.

Actually, they are always on exactly the same page. Both suffer from the same thing, and it's killing them and their marriage. More than anything else, Bill and Sarah want to feel valued, respected, appreciated, and truly loved. They both want to feel a sense of certainty in their marriage.

They just don't know they are on the same page because their individual needs for feeling those things look very different. Since they appear so starkly different to each other, their only option is to place blame and sulk away in resentment – for another six months.

Why It's Not about The Sex

Bill and Sarah's relationship had a very steamy beginning. With a strong physical attraction and desire for each other, their first year together was full of the kind of sexual intimacy that kept their cups running over. They didn't spend much time developing deeper emotional, intellectual, or spiritual connections. In fact, those were uncomfortable, scary places to be avoided at all costs. They preferred to keep things light and fun. Sex was the familiar, easy road to feel valued, respected, appreciated, and loved.

Until it wasn't any longer.

Not long into their marriage they both started to feel empty and disconnected. Sarah wanted to feel the spark of attraction, aliveness, and trust she felt at the start. Bill wanted to feel her unconditional desire, admiration, and respect he thought would never fade.

As the intensity of their early attraction waned so did their ability to be light and fun with each other. Feeling happy and in love was supposed to be easy, however, it was getting harder. They both started to question if they ever really loved each other.

They judged the depth of their love by their individual feelings of "happiness." They took no responsibility for creating love because they knew little about how to love. And the little they did know was way too risky – way too scary. So, without any other tools to dig deeper, they just stood their ground, not knowing how to give what the other needed.

Sarah wanted to be treated better.

Bill wanted more sex.

In six months, they'll have another conversation. The same conversation.

Are You Avoiding The Deep End?

The "deep end" is all about deciding to learn how to love one another. It's about Bill and Sarah trading in their "How happy am I?" measuring sticks for one that measures how well they create love. They have to want to learn how to love more than they want the other to make them happy. They must consciously decide to change their measuring stick!

Why? Because a person who is stuck in the "How happy am I?" mode of measurement is blinded by their self-interests. They are giving up responsibility for their own happiness. When they give up that responsibility, they also give up their power to think, say, and do anything that creates feelings of love in their partner.

This is the challenge for Bill and Sarah. They both need to switch their focus from feeling happy and in love to creating happiness and creating love.

Bill needs to go into the scary place of discovering what emotional intimacy and safety means for Sarah. He has to want to become a man and husband who learns how Sarah's needs for attraction and trust are met. Then he needs to turn his knowledge into action.

Sarah needs to face her fear of being more vulnerable and comfortable in creating sexual polarity. She has to want to become a woman and wife who learns how Bill's needs for admiration and desire are filled in many ways beyond sex. Then she needs to step into her fear and take action.

Bill and Sarah's unproductive, semi-annual conversations need to be replaced by something much deeper. They need to discover the joy and confidence in becoming partners who want to create love with each other. Then they will find where happiness, trust, respect, and good sex really come from.

How To Be A "Wife Whisperer" – Lessons From A Master Horse Trainer

How patience, insight and compassion can change your marriage.

The crowd laughed nervously as they watched a demonstration that would likely end in death.

One of the world's most revered and accomplished horse communicators (aka, the Horse Whisperer), Marty Marten, was showing them how to get a young, frightened, aggressive mare into a trailer. It was a narrow, two-horse, straight loading "shotgun" trailer – the worst possible option for this demonstration.

It was certain Marty would fail and possibly die in the process. Having seen Marty teach men and women his secrets over the years, I gave him at least 50-50 odds.

Running and pulling frantically at the end of the rope, the mare's eyes bulged with fear and mistrust. But Marty was unaffected. His gentle voice and soft hands guided her through a number of small requests designed to help her relax and trust him.

As her eyes softened Marty guided her toward the trailer and invited her to put just one foot inside. The crowd gasped as she suddenly blew up and ran away again throwing a kick at Marty's head. Breathing heavily, she glared at him with defiant eyes.

The mare began to sweat. It was only five minutes into the demonstration and the crowd had doubts. Some decided to leave. They had already given up on the impossible.

Marty continued his calm, deliberate approach over and over. He smiled at the mare and spoke gently. He responded to her every reaction with purposeful intent. Marty seemed to know something that nobody in the crowd knew.

At the 20-minute mark, an eternity for most people, something amazing happened. The mare put one foot in the trailer. Then one foot out. Then two feet in. And two feet out. Marty continued allowing her to learn at her own pace so she could enter and leave the trailer. She was safe. She became relaxed.

The crowd, now half its original size, erupted in applause when Marty stood inside the trailer with the happy mare, softly stroking her neck. She had found safety and relaxation. She found it in the trailer with Marty, and she was happy to be there.

A woman in the crowd yelled out her burning question. "Marty, how in the world did you do that!?

Nobody thought that horse was going in that trailer."

In his typical "less is more" style, Marty answered, "There are two reasons she went into the trailer. First, I knew beyond any doubt in my mind that she would go in. Second, she knew that I knew that."

The woman beamed and nodded as if she instantly knew what he meant.

He continued. "I know how much I respect and admire her. I know why she is unsure and distrustful. I know how her fear feels. I know how she was abused a year ago. And I know how she needs me to treat her in order to relax and trust me. All I needed to do was provide her what she needed and she would go in the trailer on her own – on her terms. She knew that I knew she would be safe and happy in the trailer."

Another man said, "I can't believe you did it in only 20 minutes."

Marty replied, "And half of the crowd has left. When you don't know what you're doing, it's easy to get impatient and give up."

I had a men's retreat at my little ranch recently, and a man made an observation during my "empathy demonstration" with Chief, my 24-year-old Appaloosa.

"You know", he said, "sometimes I'm the one who feels like the horse. Some days, I'm scared. I want to be understood. I want my wife to calmly reassure me and help me relax. I want to know that she knows we're okay and that I'm okay." I want to know that she understands and wants to meet my needs."

"That sounds awesome," I replied. "I want a woman like that, too. All of us deserve women like that."

Another man named Allen said, "Yeah, I want my wife to "whisper me" sometimes, too. But from what I'm seeing it goes both ways. It's like we're at a standoff waiting for the other to take the reins."

I asked Allen, "When it comes to your wife, what do you think she knows you know?"

He was silent for about 30 seconds, which felt like an eternity to the other men waiting for his answer.

He finally said, "I've never said this out loud before, so it feels weird. I think my wife knows that I know I'm afraid of her. She knows that I question my love for her and if we'll last. She knows that I'm terrified of losing her.

"She knows that I need her to make me feel good about myself, and that I don't know how to respond to her when she is upset or angry. She knows I'm not sure how to give her what she wants to feel from me. She knows that I'm feeling like giving up."

Another man, in the middle of a divorce, put a hand on Allen's shoulder and said, "So, what are you going to do about what she knows, bro?"

One of the biggest challenges in our relationships is knowing where we stand, what we believe and who we will be. Our partners always reflect what they experience with us. We need to learn how to show up with clarity, confidence, and love. When we are unclear, uncertain, and uncommitted our partners have no choice but to react accordingly.

The lessons Marty Marten gave in this story apply equally to husbands and wives. My work with men is to help them powerfully show up to the world and with women in order to confidently create the life and love they deserve.

How To Ride Your Husband Like A Lady

How to take the reins in your marriage and create an environment that's more fun for both of you.

"Ladies are naturally better with horses than men. They've got softer hands."

"What do you mean?" I asked the leather-faced trainer who was studying how a woman calmly gilded her horse around the corral.

"When it comes to listening to what the horse is communicating, women seem to have a better connection. They don't apply unnecessary pressure with the reins or with their legs. They tend to relate to the horse's need for space and freedom. At the same time, they manage to form an understanding – a partnership where they both get what they need. They're not hard on the bit like most guys I train. They've got soft hands. Horses respond well to that."

"Is that how your wife treats you?" I asked with a chuckle.

He squinted in the late day sun and mumbled, "Don't get me started, son."

I Like The Way You Ride Me

I told my girlfriend recently, "I like the way you ride me."

My longtime horse-girl looked at me sideways. "Oh yeah? What are you talking about?"

"Not that way. I mean you've got soft hands. I see plenty of times when you could try to pull me back, correct me, speed me up, or slow me down … but you don't. You give me my head most of time, and I like it. It feels easy. Like you trust me. It feels good."

"Most of the time?"

"Yeah. Sometimes you give me the slightest cue when I'm doing something stupid or dangerous. Like the way you always want me to wear gloves, drink more water, get to bed earlier, and avoid speeding tickets."

"It doesn't always work."

"Yeah, but I really appreciate the effort, and I notice the gentle way you do it. It makes me want to do those things. I've gotten better, you know?"

"Did you drink enough water today?"

"Umm ... no. I was too busy splitting wood at midnight without gloves."

"You boys."

The Metaphor Goes Both Ways

"Riding like a lady" simply means treating a horse with dignity, respect, kindness, and consideration for how it likes to be handled.

It means being aware of how pressure feels to the horse and how to communicate in ways that don't threaten or intimidate. A skilled rider learns how to show respect for the horse's natural need for independence and freedom from domination. She creates an environment ripe for partnership and collaboration. And fun!

Men love a woman who knows how to do this. And vice-versa, of course.

How To Be A Better Husband Or Wife Whisperer

The single defining factor in learning to effectively communicate with horses is this: You have to actually want to learn.

You also have to accept one more crucially important fact: The horse reacts to you. Period. Everything a horse does in relationship to a person is a reaction to how that person think, speaks, and acts.

Horses instinctively react to the character and intention of the person in front of them. If a person can't accept that, they should avoid relationships with horses.

In her Understanding Men coaching programs, Alison Armstrong reveals how her life with men changed for the better the day she decided to operate from the assumption that men react to her. She also decided she wanted to learn more about men and masculinity and how to be a better partner. Alison has changed thousands of lives with this message.

I teach men the same thing in reverse. You don't have to believe it's scientifically true, but pretending it is true can be empowering.

Just like with horses, your confidence soars when you start experiencing positive responses to your efforts to connect with your partner. It makes you want to learn more.

And guess what happens when two people do this at the same time?

Good stuff. Fun Stuff. That's what.

It's The Perspective That Counts

The horse analogy is meant to be a mnemonic. If it helps you to remember how much influence you have in your relationship, I've done my job.

Nearly all relationship problems are caused by how someone feels they are being treated. Each of us is one-half of the relationship equation. But we have 100% control over our own behavior and how we show up. We can spend our time complaining about how we want to be treated. Or we can adopt a new perspective that drives us to take ownership of the environment we create.

You can start with soft hands, respect, partnership, and fun.

Ride 'em cowgirl/boy.

Chapter 9
FEAR OF HITTING THE WALL –
HOW TO HANDLE THE FEAR OF
DIVORCE

> "Bottom line is ... even if you see 'em coming, you're really not ready for the big
> moments. No one asks for their life to change, not really. Yet it always does. So,
> what are we ... Helpless? Puppets? No! The big moments are still gonna come. You
> can't help this at all. What counts is what you do afterwards. This is when you find
> out who you really are."
> ~JOSS WHEDON

Your fear of divorce will sometimes be the final cause of divorce. Your wife experiences your fear of divorce and your fear of her as an unattractive, repulsive energy. Your fear makes it hard for your wife to trust and respect you. Therefore, it's hard for her to follow your lead toward improving anything in your marriage. Fear makes you play small and avoid doing anything that might rock the boat. This means you may be avoiding doing the very things your marriage needs most. This is a time for radical honesty, bold communication, and inspired action. Trust and respect can be rebuilt from a new energy of clarity, confidence, and outcome independence. This chapter will help you see yourself and your role in a new light.

John Tries To Save His Marriage. Jane Isn't Buying It

John just gave Jane the speech of his lifetime. Jane isn't buying it. Then John asks the wrong question.

John and Jane just had a possible turning point in their marriage. After another nasty exchange, John decided to finally stand up for himself and deliver a speech that came right from his heart. He fearlessly spoke his truth for the first time ever in their marriage. It was bold and it felt good.

But he has made a common mistake. John secretly thought his speech was so good that Jane would respond just as he wanted. He imagined her falling into his arms and crying. Then she would say how much she loved him and that she was sorry. John pictured her saying that she wants more respect, love, and passion, too. They'd kiss make the kind of love they used to make. They would fall asleep with entangled bodies and big smiles on their faces.

Then John woke up.

"Screw you!" Jane said. "Aren't you all Mr. Cool and Calm now. This is all your fault, you know. I don't know if I can ever trust you. I'm grabbing my pillow and sleeping on the couch."

John liked his imaginary version of the story much better.

Man, he thought. What did I do wrong?"

Then he made a common mistake and sent me an email with the title "Dude, this isn't working."

Why Isn't This Working?

"Wrong question," I told John.

"What do you mean?" he responded. "I told her my truth. I was hoping for a better reaction than that!"

"I was afraid of that. Remember, we talked about your expectations," I said. "John, "why isn't this working?" is the wrong question, because this is not about making something "work." You're not trying to manipulate her. Your talk with Jane was not some magical cog meant to fix her or your marriage.

"When you decided to speak your truth," I continued, "you did it for one reason only. You wanted to clearly communicate for yourself and to Jane what your values are. Your speech was nothing more than a declaration of your love and what you want for your marriage. You set a boundary for how you want to treat her and how you expect to be treated. You invited her to join you. Your mistake is being attached to an anticipated reaction and believing you could "fix" her and her anger. You can't."

John replied, "Well, it sucked. All I wanted was to feel a little effort on her part. A little reciprocation."

"I know," I said. "That would have been nice, but you have control over her reaction. Jane could have made herself throw you a bone to help you feel better, but she cannot make herself want to do it. The only power you have in this situation is clearly and unapologetically stating what you want and what you expect. You let her know what is non-negotiable for you in your marriage. The only control you have is in how you choose to think, speak and act from this point forward."

What If She Never Wants To Do It?

John pressed on. "I know I can't make her want to stay with me. But what if she never comes around?"

"What if?" I asked.

"That would be the worst," he said. "We would continue to be miserable and probably end up divorced."

"And then what?" I asked.

Clearly frustrated, John replied, "Then we would end up like half of our friends. The kids would suffer, and we both would wind up worse off financially. It just doesn't have to end that way! She can help me save this if she wants to."

"And what if you find out she just doesn't want to?" I asked.

Now nearly in tears, John said, "Then I would have failed as a man and husband. I would have failed as a father. And I'll probably end up alone and never see my kids. That's the scary part."

"So, you think your feelings of success and adequacy as a man, husband, and father are under the direct control of a woman who has been disrespectful, dismissive, and disinterested in you. You feel that your value and well-being as a man are measured by the level of Jane's approval of you and her willingness to be intimate again with you. Do I have that right?"

"It actually feels worse when you put it that way," John answered.

"Worse than what?" I asked.

John chuckled. "The idea of her leaving me doesn't feel as nearly as bad as my knowing that I'm letting her make me feel like such a spineless, undesirable, pathetic loser."

"One last question," I said. "No matter what Jane decides to do with her life, what are the chances of you winding up as a spineless, undesirable, pathetic loser?"

"Nearly zero," he grinned. "I can do better. I deserve better. But I still love her, you know?"

"Yes, I know, buddy."

John's Next Steps

John now has a clearer glimpse into the mindset he needs to move forward. This is a man's mojo. It's a feeling of strength, clarity, and confidence.

A man with these qualities is much better poised to deal with himself and his relationship. He responds to the stress with a clear head instead of reacting like the 15-year-old boy inside him. His decisions and responses can come from a place of strength and love for himself and his marriage.

Will a new mindset "save his marriage?" There is no way to know. It sounds like the old marriage doesn't need to be saved.

John's new mindset will help him learn how to create something new. Only Jane can decide if she wants to be a part of that.

See Jane Threaten Divorce Again. What Should John Do This Time?

When Jane repeats a familiar threat, John says something that even surprised him.

It's 10:30 a.m., and Jane and John have been texting each other madly since the big blow up at 5:30 that morning. They have both gone to work but are still arguing through their phones.

John is pursuing an apology and a truce after Jane's disrespectful outburst. Jane is defending herself and justifying her harsh words and blaming him for making her so angry.

John is feeling hurt by Jane's continual criticism and lack of affection. She's been acting cold toward him and continues to reject his efforts to reconnect.

Their emotional cyber-fight is not going well.

John: You were horrible to me this morning for no reason. You need to apologize.

Jane: Maybe I wouldn't be so horrible if I felt like I didn't have to do EVERYTHING.

John: You don't have to. I think you just want everything done YOUR way. I'm always willing to help, and you know it. But nothing I do is ever good enough for you.

Jane: With the way you try to help, I'd be better off as a single mother.

John: WTF does THAT mean. What are you saying?

Jane: Maybe it's time we get serious about just calling it quits. I'm so done with all this crap. I can't take it anymore. I think I should just leave and get it over with.

John: [silence]

Jane threatened John with divorce, again. It's her "go to" move to shut him down and silence him. It works every time, and he hates that he can't respond to it. Why? Because it scares the crap out of him.

It feels abusive. It makes his brain freeze and his mouth inoperable. It starts the horror movies in his mind of moving away from his kids, seeing Jane with someone else, and living like an aimless, penniless gypsy.

He has no defense against the fear created by her threats. Being abandoned is one of John's biggest insecurities, and Jane knows it.

They talked about their tendency to attack each other's weak spots and, during six weeks of marriage counseling, each of them vowed to do better.

But today was not one of their better days.

How The Fear Of Divorce Can Accelerate Divorce

John's fear of divorce is part of the problem. He is so focused on all the things he doesn't want that it's all he's getting. It's like a race car driver looking at the wall and trying to avoid it at the same time. John's about to hit the wall.

John is getting more anger, more arguing, more distance, and more disrespect because that's what he is bringing to the party. His fear causes him to perpetuate the negativity by negatively reacting to Jane.

This will surely speed up the decline of his marriage. John's fear of what he doesn't want keeps him from boldly standing up for what he does want. He's afraid of what Jane will say if he tells her what he expects from their marriage.

He's scared she will reject him if he takes the lead to create a more positive, compassionate, and affectionate energy in the marriage.

He is afraid that the one and only woman in the world currently qualified to share a healthy, loving, respectful, and passionate relationship may leave him for wanting just that.

Sounds a little silly when you think about it.

John thought so, too.

John's Fearless Response To Jane

This is bullshit! he said to himself. I'm not playing this game anymore. I can't just keep my mouth shut every time she brings up divorce."

Later that night, after the kids were in bed, John sat on the couch with Jane.

He was calmer and more deliberate than she had seen in a long time and it calmed her. Then John said, "Sweetie, this day was not one of our best, and I expect to never repeat it again. We both went down a rat hole we've seen way too often. I'm better than that. We're better than that.

"I love you as my wife, my lover, and the mother of our two incredible kids. I've always loved you. It's always been you. I want us to treat each other with more respect and kindness and create the life we wanted when we first met. I want the joy, affection, and tenderness back. I want more passion. I expect those things from myself and for myself.

"That's the life I intend to have – even if you divorce me. I don't want that, and I want your threats of leaving to stop. They no longer scare me, and they will destroy any chance we have of rebuilding the trust needed to move forward. I plan to lead the way. You can join me or not. And, if you really think you want a divorce, please just skip the threats, and go ahead and get the papers. I'll never try to keep you where you're not happy.

"Let's go to bed and try again tomorrow. It will be better than today … promise."

You may wonder how Jane responded. You may want to know how the story ends.

It doesn't matter. It's not the point.

John has finally become detached from his fear. He stated his intent to Jane and to the world. He is no longer dependent on the outcome with Jane, and he realizes that the only way he will ever have what he wants is to create it.

It starts with him. And he's good with that.

See Jane Get Angry. Watch John Make This Common Mistake

Jane is angry. John is about to make a big mistake. What should John do instead?

Here is the scene. It's 5:30 Monday morning, and John and Jane are back into their normal weekday routine. With jobs, kids, and pets, their mornings are usually a little hectic.

Jane: I really need your help this morning. I have to leave early because my boss called a surprise meeting today. I hate it when he does that on Mondays. I slept like crap, too.

John: Okay. No problem. I'll get the kids going and make lunches. What else do you need?

Jane: I hate when you do that.

John: Do what?

Jane: You should know what else I need. They're your kids, too. You shouldn't have to ask me how to help out with that.

John: I know how to take care of the kids. I was just asking you what else I could do to help.

Jane: That's what I'm talking about. You're just clueless in the mornings, and I feel like I've got to organize everything and make all the decisions. Never mind. I don't need your help with anything if I can't count on you.

John: Clueless? Holy crap. What's the matter with you? What did I do to deserve being talked to like that? Did you wake up on the wrong side of the bed or something?

You know how it goes from here. And it's not pretty.

What is the mistake John made? It happens all the time, and it is the number one issue I see with men facing relationship conflict like this. John's mistake was that he took the whole conversation personally.

Don't Take It Personally

This is so easy to say yet so hard to do.

John's reaction to Jane came from a dark place that many men can relate to. It's not just this 30-second discussion that has him feeling defensive and mad. He has been storing up quite a bit of resentment lately.

Jane used the word "clueless" twice on Sunday when talking about the plumbing repairs. She's been dismissive for days and told him to get "his head out of his butt" on Saturday morning.

John has been hearing a lot of "You always" and "You never" attacks.

They haven't had sex for four weeks.

It's hard to not take everything personally when his heart is telling him it feels so personal, but his feelings are steering him in the wrong direction.

John is in need of a mindset overhaul.

Think About This Differently And You Will Feel Differently

I've worked with many "Johns." I've been John. Nothing in his relationship will change if he cannot choose to think differently about what is really going on. The hurt feelings, disrespect, resentment, and emotional distance will continue. These emotions will slowly tie themselves into a knot in John's gut, which makes him question if it's all worth it.

The cause? Stinkin' thinkin'. Here's the truth about what's going on. John's thoughts aren't true, but he doesn't see it.

If he can just begin to see the truth, John will start feeling more confident and able to respond better to Jane.

What's The Truth About John?

John and I talked for weeks. We designed a new pair of "glasses" for him. He began seeing things very differently, and I asked him to write down his new truth.

John's Truth

"I've always thought angry women were angry at me. I've always thought it was my fault and my job to fix something when women were angry. I believed there was something wrong with me. The truth is that I can't own or control their anger.

"I'm not clueless, and I don't live with my head up my butt. I've accomplished incredible things professionally that most men can't even understand. I can learn how to better empathize with my wife and communicate with her in ways that support our marriage and don't result in me being a victim.

"When Jane treats me badly it doesn't mean I've screwed up. It is not all about me, and I shouldn't see it that way. I feel less defensive and more connected with her when I see why she is feeling stressed "and overwhelmed. I can respond more positively without feeling beaten up.

"I own the knot in my gut. I put it there – not Jane. My feelings of anger, resentment, and powerlessness came when I believed I had no control over her and the situation. I don't need to control her or the situation. But I can control how I think about and respond to her anger."

Don't take it personally. It's so easy to say yet so hard to do.

I think the difficulty lies in our thoughts. Our thoughts create our feelings. When we give others the power to tie knots in our guts, we will always take things personally.

The key is to find our truth and respond from a new place of self-respect and confidence. It's only from there we can share authentic love, support, and strength with our partner.

And in most cases, that's all she ever wanted anyway.

The Tool You Need Most To Fix Your Broken Relationship

A missing link revealed for many men who are struggling in their marriage.

It's been said there are no atheists in foxholes. This implies that, under extremely stressful conditions, everyone starts looking to a higher power for help or guidance.

Not everyone.

When my marriage turned horribly painful and stressful I sure wasn't looking toward religion or any type of spiritual connection for help. I was too busy trying to fix things. I didn't need any stinkin' "spiritual help."

I used my intellect to analyze and understand things. I dissected everything she did and said and planned a counter argument that would surely convince her she was wrong.

With hard work and focus, I knew I could change her feelings and stop the darkness and fear surrounding me.

Who needs spirituality when you've got the tools of logic, analysis, and a good work ethic?

You do. That's who. And I do, too. Every man I've worked with who has successfully battled through the darkness of a struggling marriage has done so because he developed spiritual clarity.

Some guys develop the strength and compassion to create a loving and inspiring new relationship with their wife. Other men move on with confidence and optimism to create an amazing and fulfilling relationship with someone new. Neither outcome would be possible if they did not achieve spiritual clarity.0

What Do I Mean By Spiritual Clarity?

I'm talking about an emotionally powerful and inspiring belief that you are meant to have a fulfilling and passionate life.

I'm talking about an unshakable faith that you were born with a purpose you deserve to fulfill. A purpose the universe needs you to fulfill.

I'm talking about an irresistible, non-negotiable vision which pulls you to live the loving, engaged, and connected life you know you want to live before it's too late.

If you do not have spiritual clarity, you are likely to feel stuck. The twisted knot in your gut and daily frustrations linger indefinitely.

Without spiritual clarity, you continue to think, say, and do things that sabotage your efforts to have what you really want. Negativity, blame, and anger dominate you. Your relationship gets worse.

Without spiritual clarity, you believe every negative thing you think and hear is true. And you react with resentment and contempt that pull you further into the downward spiral you're fighting against. You stay stuck and keep thinking you are doomed to unhappiness.

In her book *Confidence: Finding It and Living It*, Dr. Barbara DeAngelis beautifully explains the importance of Emotional Confidence, Behavioral Confidence, and Spiritual Confidence. She makes a compelling case for why spiritual clarity is so important. It must precede the first two.

Emotional Confidence is the clarity and values that drive what we think and feel about events in our life.

Behavioral Confidence is the clarity and values that drive how we choose to respond to those events.

Spiritual Confidence is the foundation supporting our ability to think, feel and respond in the ways that honor ourselves and our values.

With a strong belief about the life you are meant to have you can stop taking things so personally. You know the pain won't last forever, and you can choose to face it more productively. If you believe you will have the love, respect, affection, trust, and intimacy you want, then your pain today is just a stepping-stone.

With faith in your purpose you know what you deserve, and you fight boldly against the negative forces pulling you from that purpose. You are unafraid to speak your mind and defend your values from a place of love instead of anger.

With a compelling vision of your future, you courageously pursue the life and relationship you want, and you create the environment necessary to have it. You hold yourself accountable to higher standards because you want to, and it is only men with those standards who get what they want.

In my coaching practice, I spend a lot of time helping a man get crystal clear. He becomes unapologetic in asking for what he wants and stating what he expects. He is emotionally confident and responds to frustration with clarity, strength, compassion, and empathy. He declares a stronger set of values and personal accountability for being a man who is proud of himself.

He no longer tries to analyze his wife or tries to make her happy all the time. He stops walking on eggshells in his own home. He is confident in who he is being and how he behaves. All of those things are extremely hard to do if he has no sense of why he wants those things.

Are you clear about your why? It lives in the land of your spiritual clarity. You have to go there first before you can confidently think, feel, and act like a man who creates the life and relationship he deserves.

Deciding What To Do With Your Marriage?

Why do we believe the solution to an unhappy marriage is to fix or replace your spouse?

So, there it is.

The question that has been in your head for quite some time now.

Maybe you've never said it out loud before or have seen it in writing.

Maybe you've secretly talked about it with your therapist, your mom, your friends, or even your lover. This question causes some of the most painful thinking and talking a person can imagine. There's a really good reason for that.

"What should I do about my marriage?" is a trick question. The question implies that the marriage is as detached from you as a leaky faucet or tired old car. Those things have gone bad on their own without your involvement. The decision to fix or replace them can be a nagging and difficult one. But, in the end, it's just a matter of time and/or money.

Most people view their troubled marriage much the same way. It seems to be an autonomous entity that either works or doesn't. It should be easily fixable or replaceable. Therein lies the trick. It's not.

Why Do We Believe The Solution To An Unhealthy Marriage Is To Fix Or Replace Our Spouse?

Maybe it's not our spouse, exactly. Maybe it's fixing or replacing the house, the in-laws, the job, or the lifestyle. Maybe, if there was more money, less stress, more free time, more sex, or more respect, everything would smooth out. Maybe, if all the variables around us could align just so, then we would finally achieve the level of trust, respect, happiness, love, and passion we think we deserve.

The trick question implies that we might have some control over the marriage or spousal "beast" to have those needs met the way we want them met. The trick question implies that the decision can actually be made without including ourselves as part of the problem.

It's the wrong question. The only rational and actionable question is, "What to do about myself in this marriage?"

That is the right question.

The Truth Hurts

There is a pain associated with asking the right question. A very real pain.

It's the pain of realizing that our ability to directly influence the outcome of our marriage is out of our control. It's the pain of guilt inflicted stomach knots when we are faced with acknowledging our own contributions to an unhealthy marriage. It's the pain of coming to terms with the fact that we have no power over the choices of other people.

It's this pain which causes so many of us to focus our attention elsewhere and ask the wrong questions. However, by asking the right question, you can finally and clearly see the things you can control. And the good news is that it is only those things that have a chance at improving your relationship with anyone – including your spouse.

The Things You Can Control

The things you can control do not include changing anyone but you. The things you can control will not automatically improve your marriage. But the things you can control will immediately start changing the energy in your marriage. It is the nature of the environment that you choose to create and live in that determines the choices of others close to you.

If you want your spouse to join you in a healthier and happier marriage, the changes you choose to make in yourself must match the environment you desire. There is no guarantee that the changes you make will improve or save your marriage. Remember, that is out of your hands. However, those changes will improve or save you.

The changes you make must be for you only because that is who you choose to be, for this or any relationship. That is all you can control. Your spouse gets to make their choices accordingly.

If you are the smart, loving, strong, and generous person you think you are, then this should be easy, right? I can tell you it is not. It's work. Like any good thing in your life, it's worth working for! We're never as good as we think we are.

So, what do these changes look like? How do you know what to do or how to do it? These are very personal choices you must make on your own.

Do Any Of These Feel Right For You?

Here are a few of the personal change values some of my married

clients have select to adopt and live by:

Personal Change Values

- When I speak to my spouse my intention will always be from a place of love.
- I will always handle conflicts with the goal of making my spouse feel my respect.
- I will work on choosing healthy responses instead of destructive reactions to stress.
- I will learn what my spouse's real emotional needs are and begin to meet those needs without judgement or conditions.
- I will make any boundaries clear for bad martial behavior and live by those standards each day.
- I will not apologize for being a passionate, sexual person or for my intention to enjoy those gifts in my life.
- I will stop acting with judgment, resentment, or disappointment and will stop taking everything personally.
- I can't control the choices my spouse makes, but I will invite them to enjoy our marriage based on healthy shared values.

These are just a few of the types of changes a partner can choose

to make no matter what anybody else thinks or does in response.

They are for you and you alone.

A choice to make these changes is a commitment to yourself.

You may need some help or encouragement from a professional

counselor or life coach. It is some of the most valuable and important

work you can do. Consistency is extremely important. It might

improve or save your marriage. It might not but it is the only chance

you have.

What Now?

Make a choice. Make a decision. Start the process of talking this out with someone you trust. Talk with a close friend, mentor, counselor – it doesn't matter. Talking to someone else helps you hold yourself accountable for making the change you want to make in life.

It doesn't mean you have to get all sappy and tell them you want to change your life around. You can if you want, but the point is to simply hold yourself accountable for the change you want to make in order to have extra motivation to follow through with the commitments you make to yourself.

Also, a close friend, counselor, etc. can help you by detailing what they see and when you're succeeding or missing the boat on certain goals you're trying to obtain. They'll help you make sure you're not treating your marriage like some old faucet that's disposable.

When you start to recognize that your spouse isn't the only contributor to your problems and also realize that you can unilaterally influence your happiness in your marriage with or without your spouse, that's when you have real power in your relationship. Then, and only then, can you make a truly informed

decision about what to do with your marriage.

Chapter 10

WHEN YOU HIT THE WALL – WHAT TO DO WHEN DIVORCE SEEMS CERTAIN

> "Sometimes good things fall apart so better things can fall together."
> ~MARILYN MONROE

Divorce happens. Unless you've been living in a cave you know that each attempt at marriage has nearly a 50/50 shot of working out in the long run. That was true on your wedding day, and it's true right now. I realize the statistics don't help you feel any better, because it now appears the coin flip didn't go your way.

What should you be thinking? What happens next? What does this mean about me as a man? What does the future hold? This are questions you might be asking now. This chapter provides you some insight and hope about what's next.

Bottom line: You're going to be just fine, if you make the right choices.

Three Clear Clues Your Marriage Isn't Worth Saving

What you can do instead of trying to save a marriage you don't want.

There are some things just not worth fighting for, and one of those is a marriage totally devoid of the most basic elements of an intimate relationship. Why would you fight for a marriage full of disrespect? Why would you hold on to a relationship where kindness is held in contempt? Why would you want to save a romantic partnership without even the smallest crumbs of affection?

Yet, many of the unhappily married men I meet are doing just that. They are desperately clinging on to their crumbling marriage and clutching their disconnected partner with a death grip. And it's making matters worse every day.

You're Not Gonna Die

I'm here to tell you that you won't die. It's okay to let go. In fact, you will actually start to thrive when you learn to stop fighting for the wrong things. You've been fighting to save a relationship full of all the things you don't want. That relationship is not worth saving!

I'm not talking about divorce. I'm talking about letting this version of your life and marriage die. Only then will you be able to gather the clarity, confidence, and strength to fight for what you really do want. Hopefully, you can create that with her … if she wants the same things.

You'll never get the good things you want in your relationship until you drop the bad things that have gotten you to this point. And, no, you do not need anyone's help to do this. Not even hers.

Three Clues It's Time To Let This Marriage Die

It's painful to watch men struggling to save something they don't even want. The reason they do this is because they don't know how to create what they do want. Here are the top three clues your current marriage situation must be allowed to die.

1. You don't treat each other with respect.
2. You don't treat each other with kindness.
3. You don't give each other emotional or physical affection.

Admit it. You don't want any of those any longer. You hate it when you feel it from her, and you hate it when you feel it coming from yourself. You may think it's impossible to let those things die if she won't play along. You may think you're doomed to a disrespectful, mean-spirited, unaffectionate life. And you would be wrong. You can create whatever the hell it is you want, and you don't need anybody's cooperation or permission to do this.

How? You make the incredibly simple decision that, starting today – not tomorrow – that you are a man of respect, kindness, and affection.

There. Done. Easy-peasy.

Now ... start acting that way. Begin creating what you want by consistently modeling what you want. Quit blaming anyone else in the world for you not being a respectful, kind, and affectionate man who lives a respectful, kind, and affectionate life!

What A Respectful, Kind, Affectionate Man Looks Like

You don't have to tell me how hard this is going to be. This would be simple if you didn't have someone living with you who may not trust or believe that you're actually a respectful, kind, affectionate man. Overall, when someone doesn't trust or believe you are who you think you are, sometimes you'll agree with them. Don't do that.

Trust yourself. Believe in yourself. Without that, you're sunk no

matter what happens.

Here are some examples of what it might look like when you trust

and believe in yourself.

Respect
- Be calm and deliberate when speaking. Check your emotions. Listen and respond.
- Try to understand more than you need to be understood. Patience. Lose urgency in being "right."
- Lose the agenda for what you think she should be giving you. Give first – receive second.
- Support her as an individual before you try to hold her accountable for being your perfect partner.
- Respectful men communicate from a place of love and empathy – consistently.

Kindness
- Make kindness and consideration a choice from your heart – not part of a subliminal negotiation.
- Empathize with her bad moods and feeling, though you don't have to copy them.
- Be fearless in saying kind things and doing kind deeds. Kind men don't care if their kindness is welcomed or not.
- Respond to conflict with an unwavering intention of kindness. Consistency creates trust.
- Kind men don't require others to be kind to them. Kind men don't give a f*ck.

Affection
- Give compliments, hugs, kisses, pats, touches, and mushy-mushy talk at will. Learn to enjoy your affectionate nature without requiring it first from others.
- Fearlessly show appreciation and gratitude without expectations.
- Boldly invite her into intimacy of all types without expectations. "No" is always her option, but affectionate men don't allow "No" to shut down their affectionate nature.
- Allow your sensual interactions to remain sensual. Show some restraint as you milk the sweetness of non-sexual intimacy. All-day foreplay is an end in itself.
- Be shamelessly proud of your masculine sexuality and your desire for her.

Why This Is So Hard For Men

I know reading list after list of what to do better can be annoying. It's annoying because, if it were that simple to create a respectful, kind, and affectionate relationship, you would have done it by now.

Why is it so hard for us men to do? Because we don't know exactly how to do it. Couple that with a few decades of shame, guilt, and fear … well, I may as well be telling you how to fly an F-15 in three easy steps. Nevertheless, it's really not that hard once you learn to trust and believe in yourself.

Most of us were never taught how to be self-reliant, confident, unapologetic men. So, when we make our attempts at being respectful, kind, and considerate we come across as uncertain, tentative, and weak. And it's that fearful energy that creates all our problems.

It's impossible to create anything we want when we're operating from fear. We fear what people will think, say, or do. We fear not getting the outcome we want. We fear the consequences of being who we really want to be. We fear not being loved anymore … maybe forever.

If you want to create a whole new version of your life and marriage, your first order of business is to face and then conquer these fears. Men who do this work quickly find out they can create whatever they want.

Predicting The End Of Your Marriage Two Years Before

A lot of couples are painfully unaware of this two-year warning clock in their marriage.

I thought I was all alone. I thought I was special. But, over the years, my clients have proved me wrong. This happens nearly every day.

There is a very definite trend with marriages that end with the man left standing in shock and awe.

"I Didn't see it coming."

"How could she be so cold?"

"Wait! I can change!"

"We can fix this! Can't we?"

The Alarming Trend

In almost every case where a woman has initiated divorce, I've discovered a common thread. And when I present this information to a group of divorced women they sheepishly nod in agreement.

The alarming trend is that nearly all of them knew they would be getting divorced about 24 months before it happened. The funny thing is, they didn't really know this consciously until the two-year clock had run out.

I asked one of them, "How did you know?"

She said, "My heart just told me so."

She went on to explain about the time leading up to the start of the two-year warning clock. She said she tried to communicate her feelings, her fears, and her dreams. She said she felt disappointed with their relationship, how they treated each other, and the quality of their intimate life. She said she felt more and more like she didn't matter and wasn't valued.

She wanted more connection, more love, and more fun. She thought she was as direct as possible in explaining it all to her husband. He just didn't seem to hear it or want to hear it.

She felt like she started out in her marriage like a brightly lit office building bustling with hope and opportunity. But she slowly felt like the office lights were being turned off – one by one. Every year saw another light go out. By the time her two-year warning clock started she felt dark. She was checked out. Emotionally numb.

She was about to spend the next two years grieving the end of her marriage in quiet solitude. But she was unprepared for the level of shock it would create in her husband.

How could he not see the darkness, the stillness, the sadness? How could he just be starting his grief when she was finally finishing hers?

Her Two-Year Warning Clock – Is It Ticking?

Once the clock starts ticking most husbands don't see much difference. This is a problem because, once it starts, it is nearly impossible to stop.

Money gets made, bills get paid, dinner parties go on, and the kids make their soccer games on time. In the house, the air is cool. Matter of fact, it's businesslike and cordial.

In the bedroom, there is still the routine of mostly lukewarm, obligatory, and unsatisfying sex. There is a little more distance and little more disdain that shows up. But it's not alarming. *It's just a phase ...* he thinks.

She may be taking trips alone with mom or sister, spending more time at work or with friends. She is unusually spunky and happy when she is with her friends – or even the dog! But she's still cool and detached in her own living room with him.

Her conversations are practical and functional. Oddly, she is less angry and has lowered her expectations. There may be fewer arguments than ever before.

Then, one day, out of grief, guilt, or desperation, she initiates lovemaking. And it will be pretty good.

Ahh ... Everything must be okay, he thinks.

Whose Fault Is This?

I'm not blaming him, and I'm not blaming her. I'm just reporting the facts here. This trend is so pervasive it needs to be revealed.

It's not just the husbands who feel clueless at the end of the ticking clock. Most of the women I've talked to didn't actually know it started. It just so happens that 24 months is about how long it takes most women to realize their heart has turned off. The lights are all off. They feel dark.

It's easy to blame him for not knowing better or for not being more attentive. And it's easy to blame her for not being more open and communicative. The truth is, neither of them knew exactly what was happening until the clock ran out and her heart spoke.

What Can You Do With This Information?

First of all, awareness is king. Just knowing this gives you a leg up because it can help you start a conversation. A real conversation full of scary, vulnerable feelings and nasty stuff like that.

Share this article with your partner – not as a threat, but as a dinner invitation. Invite her/him to "turn some lights back on" in your relationship. Explain why you love her/him and how you dream about your next 10 years together.

Show her/him you are willing to show all your cards and hold nothing back. Inspire her/him to be vulnerable with you, to talk about the reality of your relationship and what you really want to create together. Ask more questions than you give answers.

Treat her/him like a first date. It's quite possible neither of you have gotten close to trying as hard as you need to. Oh, and try to do this before the two-year clock gets started.

It gets really hard after that.

How This Man Initiated Divorce With His Honor Intact

Meet Luke. He's decided he is getting divorced. And he's going to be okay.

Luke is 47 years old, married for 19 years, two kids (15 and 17), a house, a dog, and a condo in Florida. He's been trying to save his marriage for four years.

Starting today, he is done trying and has made the decision to move on. He isn't going to complain to her again. No more threats of leaving. No more arguing. No more living in fear that the rest of his life will be miserable.

On Saturday, he will simply and calmly inform her of his decision.

Luke Is A Bit Odd

Luke is an oddball. Women initiate divorces more often than men by a factor of two to one. But Luke is a rare breed who has decided exactly how he wants his life to go and has gained the courage to take action.

He isn't leaving for another woman. He has tried to get his wife to join him in counseling without success. He has read countless books and attended seminars to help improve himself as a husband and a father. He is emotionally intelligent, available, and articulate.

After four years of personal effort and futile conversations there has been no improvement in the cold, distant, disrespectful, and indifferent attitude his wife shows toward him. It is crystal clear now to Luke that she has no desire, willingness, or capability to be the type of partner he wants and deserves in his life.

It would be different if he thought there was a chance – the slightest glimmer of hope. But his marriage is dead and, despite his efforts, she has no intention of creating a new life with him.

Saturday is the day he will begin creating his own.

Regret And Guilt

In his work to save his relationship, Luke has had plenty of time to reflect. He isn't a perfect man and he admits it. But he is a man who is willing to learn and grow. He wishes his wife were, too. He regrets several of the missteps and mistakes many young couples

241

make. He regrets being angry and confused with her. He regrets saying stupid things and being insensitive at times.

Guilt sets in each time he looks back at a period when he could have been a stronger man. More confident. More loving. More supportive. More empathetic. He wonders if she will ever feel regret or guilt for her imperfections and bad choices.

And then the big question: What if he knew then what he knows now? Would it have changed anything?

Divorcing With Honor

The conversation lasted only about 15 minutes on Saturday. She didn't have much to say.

Luke didn't ask any questions this time. He didn't wait for a rebuttal. His calm, deliberate, and kind frame of mind felt natural to him as he explained why he was ending the marriage and what the necessary next steps would be. He didn't try to dig up old pains or place blame. He simply explained the type of life and love he was going to pursue from this day forward and that it didn't include her anymore.

She cried for the first time in years. Luke had finished crying months ago.

They agreed to settle amicably and used a lawyer who specializes in mediations to help with the paperwork.

During his personal growth work Luke adopted some important rules that directed his energy. Over the next few months, he added a few more. These rules were for him and nobody else. They were his own honor code.

Luke's Honor Code

- I can't control anyone or the choices they make. I can only control how I respond.
- I am clear about my own values and beliefs. When I am clear, there is no need to argue about them or defend them.
- I invite into my life those people who share my values for healthy, respectful, caring relationships. Those who don't will not be in my life.
- I show my kids a model of a man who acts from a place of love and compassion.
- I have high expectations of myself and for the type of life I'll lead.
- I honor my wife and my marriage without placing blame or talking behind her back.
- I accept my role in our imperfect marriage and choose to use the mistakes and the pain to become a better man.

Luke's story is shared by many men I know personally. This short account doesn't show the depth of soul searching, personal exploration, emotional anguish, and sadness they experience on their way to this kind of clarity and confidence. In fact, clarity and confidence can't be achieved without a ton of work and anguish.

A decision to end your marriage shouldn't be taken lightly. In most cases, men have more work to do before they see as clearly and feel as confident as Luke.

And if you think you're ready to create a new chapter in your life, do it with your honor intact. You will never regret it.

Chapter 11
RETOOLING YOUR MOJO – HOW TO
REGAIN YOUR CONFIDENCE

> Love yourself first and everything else falls in line. You really have to love yourself
> to get anything done in this world.
> ~LUCILLE BALL

"I never used to be this guy! She took away my mojo!"

I've heard many variations of this complaint from men. They remember a time when they knew exactly who they were, what they wanted, and where they were going. Then they get married and slowly morph into a tentative man whose main concern is "keeping momma happy." They no longer have a clear, compelling vision of their future, and they feel trapped and confused about what to do next. How did this happen? How do you get out of this prison? This chapter will give you the perspective you need to help you find the guy you used to be. Being that guy in your marriage is likely what is missing most – for both of you.

Did Your Marriage Take Away Your Mojo?

The missing link revealed in a married man's mojo.

There's a heart-breaking story I hear over and over again from married men. It sounds exactly like this.

Dear Steve,

I've been reading your stuff for a while now. The way you talk about confidence, masculine power, and mojo has made me realize something. And it pisses me off!

Before I got married I WAS that guy. I was calm, relaxed, and confident with women. I didn't need women to make me feel good, and I was totally comfortable in my own skin. I had my share of beautiful women and wild nights. I never worried what they thought of me. I didn't get into arguments and I wasn't rattled by anything. I slept great. I was in great shape. I was happy. I had my swagger!

And now … I've lost it. I've lost it all.

I don't know how or why, but I feel like I'm nervous as a cat and walking on eggshells all the time. I see myself bugging my wife for attention and reassurance, and I hate what I see.

But I can't stop. I'm feeling uncertain and insecure about my marriage and myself. And I wonder if she is creating new relationships.

I walk through the door and I turn into a "mush pile."

I think I'm probably pushing her away, and I don't know how to stop.

I want the "old me" back.

Does This Sound Familiar?

If you're reading this saying, "Damn, I could have written that word for word," you are not alone. It's incredibly common for married men to feel like they've lost the mojo they once had. Why? Because the mojo they once had was a different kind of mojo!

The cocky confidence and self-reliance we feel before we're in a committed romantic relationship comes from a different place. It comes from confidence in what we're learning and the skills we are honing. "Single man mojo" (never-before married) is typically driven by feelings of competency and worthiness generated by what we know and what we do. In other words, we feel smart, capable, competent, and pleased with ourselves.

If the story above resonates with you, you're not feeling very smart, capable, competent, or pleased right now, are you? In fact, you may be feeling the opposite. Dazed, inadequate, clumsy, and unhappy might be more like it. Then sprinkle on top a little bit of anger, resentment, and blame. It's the perfect storm for making a guy wonder if it's all worth it.

Life used to be so much easier.

The Missing Link In The Married Man's Mojo

It's easy to be fooled when we're operating within our single-man mojo. We are constantly validated with attention, praise, respect, and appreciation for what we know and what we do. This applies especially at work and on dates with women who are impressed by our status, our social and financial value, and our obvious self-confidence. When we're operating in this mode, we don't have to think about who we are being.

This is because what we know and what we do has already earned us the toxic external validation we crave. This validation is our only measure of adequacy, desirability, and "good-enoughness." It's toxic because it is like cocaine for the insecure man. Without an internal source of validation, he will end up overdosing on the external validation which causes him to believe his own bullshit. He thinks he is better than he is.

Then he gets married. And he tries to play the same game. His addiction to external validation then becomes a toxic neediness. His wife can't stand it. And it makes him feel like a dazed and confused "mush pile."

Here's the missing link: The only thing that will make you feel truly capable, competent, and pleased is an indubitable awareness of your own value – that you are being the man you want to be without needing her to validate that for you.

Your romantic partner becomes quickly unimpressed by what you know and what you do. Those are slam dunks for you and she knows it. If you continue your validation seeking behavior from her she will turn away. She will feel disgusted. Even worse, she will feel uncertain about you, and she will lose her respect for you.

Your bad-ass intelligence and mad money-making skills are no longer enough. She wants to feel your unshaken commitment to being the man you're proud of. This is the only path to her feeling genuine respect and appreciation for you.

That includes being present. Being self-aware. Being empathetic. Being considerate. Being firm in your values. Being a man of your word. Being consistent.

Most importantly, it includes being a self-reliant man who operates to his own drummer no matter who watches. He has non-negotiable boundaries and is willing to stand up for himself no matter the outcome.

Bottom Line – You Can't Fill A Cup With Holes In The Bottom

Most men want attention, praise, respect, and appreciation in their marriage. We want to feel like that "cup" is topped off frequently. While we are unapologetic about wanting our partner to contribute to that cup, she can't be the primary provider.

If our cup is already "leaky" with holes of insecurity and self-doubt, she stands no chance of keeping it full. Her affection and appreciation runs out the bottom faster than she can fill it. So, we'll keep going back to her for a refill. And the effort will soon exhaust her.

We have to do the inner work necessary to provide a water-tight container of self-respect and self-affirmation. When that cup is always over half-full we feel less needy and we're able to give respect and affirmation much easier. It's the authentic giving from that cup that makes reciprocation effortless for our partner.

This is the kind of mojo I'm talking about. It's self-propelled by living in accordance with our own values and our own rules. It's not sourced from our intellect or our skill set. It comes from an unconditional, unapologetic, and crystal-clear intention of being the best version of ourselves first.

Bonus Section
THOUGHTS FOR THE POWERFUL, CONSCIOUS WOMAN

"You're more powerful than you think. In that single moment when you glance in our direction, we lock eyes, and all we feel is our heart beating through your chest, you have us. And there is absolutely nothing we can do about it!"
~ALEXANDER T. MACGREGOR

Women tend to believe the negative childhood stories they learn about what men are and what they really want. Why wouldn't they? There is an ample supply of social support for the notions of toxic masculinity, bumbling husbandry, and misdirected manhood. If a woman wants to believe the negative stories she doesn't need to look far for confirmation of her fears. And this is where marriages often go wrong. A choice to see a man in a negative light will always result in actions that create and nurture a negative reality.

I included this chapter to offer a new perspective about what men think about and what they want in marriage. What if both partners chose to reprogram their thoughts, projections, and intentions toward each other? How amazing would it feel if both men and women started assuming the best about each other?

The Surprising Secret Men Wish Their Wives Knew But Never Tell Them

This will surprise women everywhere. Men will just nod their heads in agreement.

I recently interviewed my colleague, author and men's relationship coach Karen Brody, who says most women completely misunderstand men and what they want. She conducted a survey with her subscribers and discovered one huge secret married men wish their wives knew but may never tell them.

The results may surprise women. Men? Not so much.

If you are a man who sees himself in this survey, think about why men readily tell their coaches secrets they never share with their wives. What holds us back? How would it feel to become confident enough to clearly state your feelings in ways that could improve your marriage and the way your wife feels your love?

Check out what Karen shares below. It may help empower you to see you're not alone. And it may help empower you to fearlessly share your secrets with your mate!

Steve: Karen, you obviously already know a lot about men as you coach men and wrote *Open Her* for men. What were you hoping to achieve in your survey?

Karen: My hope was to learn more about the secret lives of men – or what we women perceive as secret lives – and to acknowledge men as complex beings.

Steve: What did you discover?

Karen: That I am still learning about men! It was exciting to ask a question and not know what the answer would be. I asked, "What do you wish your female partner knew about you?" and gave them the following choices to this question:

- That you hurt, too.
- That you shoulder a lot of responsibility.
- That you aren't all about the sex.
- That you love her deeply and genuinely.

Steve: So, what surprised you?

Karen: I know that men aren't all about the sex, but, sometimes, I wonder in an anonymous survey if something different will emerge. Frankly, it never does, no matter how many ways I survey men. Yes, men love sex, but their reasons are so much more complex than women tend to think. What surprised me was the energy the men put into conveying to me, "We love our wives."

Steve: What was the number one thing men told you they wanted their partner to know about them?

Karen: I imagine you already know this, Steve. It was ... drum roll... "That you love her deeply and genuinely."

Steve: What surprised you about that response?

Karen: It clearly aligns with the men I coach — men who are extraordinary in that they want to work on being better men. What surprised me is how far reaching this sentiment is.

Steve: Why is this message important, and what's the takeaway for women?

Karen: It's important because it's a call for women to realize their men may be expressing feelings of love differently than she does. It's clear that men are struggling to get their messages of love across to their wives, and that their wives are missing the broadcasts. Women often don't hear men's expressions of love because their "love radar" is set to a different channel.

For example, I might be yearning for the kind of words that confirm me as my man's "one," as his soulmate. Meanwhile, he's pouring himself into his work to earn the money to support our dreams. I might see his efforts as not focused on me, as him "working too much," while he sees them as powerful demonstrations of his love and devotion. This is exactly how some women miss men's communications of love.

A woman might be craving the confirmation that her husband sees who she really is and loves her for who she is, while he's off studying how to be a better lover on his own, to show this to her. Again, he's making his demonstrations, they're just not what she's yearning for in her feminine heart.

When men better understand women, romantically, they're able to both give in the ways that make sense to them and fulfill their woman's needs for feminine romance. And conversely, when women better understand men and how to love them, they're able to see love being demonstrated in ways that were invisible to them before.

Steve: What were the other responses in the survey in order of popularity?

Karen: Again, based on the question "What do you wish your female partner knew about you?" these are their responses, answers two through five.

- That you shoulder a lot of responsibility.
- That you're not all about the sex.
- That you'd also like to be heard.
- That you hurt, too.
- Other

I got a lot of hand-written answers in the Other box on this question. The men clearly wanted to drive home the message, "We work really hard to make our wives happy, and we're saddened by their lack of generosity when it comes to affection and sex."

I felt them as a giant masculine chorus saying: "Your lack of desire hurts!"

Steve: Any final comments?

Karen: I was able to share the results of this survey with thousands of my women subscribers. Assisting women to understand men is deeply satisfying for me – as I work with men and love them. When women finally get that men are complex, emotionally, and sexually, they open themselves to being a lot more amorous. This moves us all in a very positive direction!

How a Woman's Finger Can Send a Man Through the Roof

The under-utilized power of a woman's little finger explained.

Women's jaws would drop if they could listen in on my conversations with married men.

Our discussions contradict just about every misconception wives utter about their husbands. Husbands don't want to hurt. They don't want to argue. They don't want to control. And they definitely don't "just want sex." These guys are desperate for her to know the truth. And they shed tears at the thought that their wife may never want to know the truth.

The Power In Her Pinky

The truth for these men lies in the end of her pinky finger. In that finger is packed an unspeakable power many wives choose to ignore or have yet to discover. It's so simple and so tender that men are afraid to even ask for it. We barely talk about it with each other! We don't want to appear soft. We don't want to risk a woman's reaction to our weakness.

What is it? It is the power of a delicate skin-to-skin touch of feminine acceptance and approval.

When a woman calmly grazes the end of her pinky finger across any part of a man's body and offers a verbal or non-verbal vote of confidence or support, his world changes at that instant. It is so powerful we are often left speechless. Our throats and tear ducts begin to swell and we quietly indulge in the comforting reassurance of the moment. If we could package the word "love" it would feel like this when the bottle was opened.

Our "well-being meter" pegs out and our heart rate and breathing slows.

Every husband I know is dying to feel this. Simple, easy-peasy feminine acceptance and approval. Nothing else. Just … this.

A World Of Men Speak About Pinky Power

These are real examples of how men across the globe describe it. In every case I can hear their clenched voice of vulnerability trying to sound "strong" as they speak. Just for fun, try to imagine their accents as you read these.

Oklahoma
"She reached over during the movie and put her hand on my knee and looked at me and smiled and said, 'I'm happy you brought us here, thank you.'"

Alberta
"She slapped me on the butt and giggled and called me 'stud' "

UK
"She scratched the top of my head for about two minutes and didn't say anything. It was awesome."

Turkey
"She touched my elbow and whispered, 'You're such a good father and a sweet man, I love that about you.' "

Jordan
"When I told her about my idea for a better vacation spot she grabbed my arm and said, 'I f#cking love you!' "

New Zealand
"She just reached across the car seat and scratched the back of my head softly as I drove. It's intoxicating."

Colorado
"She spooned her cold butt into me and said, 'Oh, baby you're always so warm.'" Okay, that one was mine.

Why Men Can't Tell Women About Pinky Power

It's simple. We think women will think it's silly. It's not "manly." Too vulnerable.

Women might laugh at the notion that their words and touch could cause a lump in our throats. Even if we try to explain it, they might just roll their eyes along with a big "Puh-lease!"

The most common reason husbands feel like they can't talk about it is because their wives have already proven they aren't interested or can't handle it.

In her brilliant article "I Am the Patriarchy," Jonalyn Grace Fincher listed 17 shining examples of how women refuse to let men be vulnerable. The article continued the discussion Brene Brown started in her book, Daring Greatly, where she addresses male vulnerability. Brown states:

"We ask men to be vulnerable, we beg them to let us in, and we plead with them to tell us when they're afraid, but the truth is that most women can't stomach it. In these moments when real vulnerability happens in men, most of us recoil with fear and that fear manifests as everything from disappointment to disgust. And men are very smart."

What most women don't know is that just reading this list can make a grown man cry. These things happen on a daily basis for many husbands who don't dare discuss them. Jonalyn's starter-kit list for women appears at the end of the article.

What To Do With This Information

For the Women:

You have more personal influence and power in your relationship than you know. Your ability to inspire feelings of confidence and well-being in your man is available to you at all times – every minute of every day. What might you stop doing today and start doing tomorrow that could change his world in an instant? You have this secret power – why wouldn't you use it?

For the Men:

Admit it. You want pinky power. You love pinky power. Her touch of approval and acceptance is a gift you want more than sex. If we're honest, those are the feelings we seek through sex, aren't they? Don't be ashamed of your needs and vulnerability. Stand proud in your manly desire for her pinky power. Explain it without apology or fear. Find out what her version of pinky power is from you. Then apply generously.

Jonalyn's Starter Kit For Women

- Believing my husband is substandard when I have to do manual labor(e.g. show shoveling) due to his absence, illness, or unavailability.
- Avoiding eye contact when he admits feeling overwhelmed.
- Taking over when he seems to fumble.
- Assuming his emotional absence (shutdown) is normal for men and refuse to pursue his feelings.
- Show embarrassment when he's afraid.
- Expect him to shoulder the hardest work (emotionally, physically, intellectually, spiritually) without complaint.
- Never ask him what he's afraid of.
- Refuse to offer him the understanding and sympathy I offer my girlfriends when he's overwhelmed.
- Expect him to tolerate more criticism than a woman.
- Grow quickly impatient when he doesn't demonstrate mastery over a project like booking social events, filing our taxes, or fixing the kitchen sink.
- Become business-like and cold when he asks for help.
- Know our girlfriend's needs and wants more than we know our own husband's.
- Hide his mistakes from our kids as if they (like me) can't hand him being vulnerable.
- Expect him to have more strength than I do.
- Expect him to shoulder more grunt work.
- Expect him to "man up" (whatever that means) when I want him to do something unpleasant.
- Expect him to inspect every scary sound in the house when you're equally trained in firearms, then call him names (even in your head) when he shows hesitation.

It's Not Just Sex That He's Longing For – It's This

What many married men secretly crave and have a hard time asking for.

Do you know why romance and sensuality novels for women are so popular? Short answer: the authors know exactly how to give women" that feeling."

That feeling has many facets, and she loves of them. She tingles with the flirtatiousness of the conversation. She blushes at the boldness and sensual innuendo. She craves the unapologetic desire. She wants to be "taken" by her man. The sexual polarity and tension has her on pins and needles of anticipation. She is aching for the climactic release from this torture.

And her husband doesn't quite get it. He reads the same passage and has a lukewarm response. Sure, it's a little titillating. But it's not the kind of "romance" language he has told me he is longing for.

He is a long-time married man who is just dying to star in a different scene. As he struggles to understand her emotional reaction to those scenes written for her, she can also be clueless about his deepest desires.

And it's not a sex scene. To him, it seems she just doesn't understand (or doesn't care?) why reading this scene will almost always bring a tear to his eye and a lump in his throat. More than anything, he wants that feeling, and only she has the power to supply that.

The Romance Story That Can Make Men Cry

They were finally alone. He had been looking forward to doing this for months and she finally agreed to a getaway for just the two of them. The kids were with grandma and they would finally have a chance to reconnect as a man and woman—not as dad and mom.

Their truck was cruising west on the hot desert highway into a beautiful sunset as one of their favorite songs from high school came on the radio. They both started humming the song and broke into the chorus at the exact same time. They both laughed and smiled without talking as the song ended.

After another few miles, she gently reached across the top of the bench seat and her hand found the back of his head. Her fingers rolled and massaged through his hair as she delivered the most loving half-scratch, half-massage treatment he hadn't felt in a long time.
He caught her looking at him out of the side of his eye and said, 'What's that look for?

She kept eye contact and grinned as she said, 'This was such a good plan. I'm so happy you're my man. Thank you for making me go on this trip. We both need this, don't we?'

As they pulled into town that night, he realized he had not even noticed the last 100 miles. While his truck found its own way, he had been traveling on Cloud Nine.

Many women reading this will think I'm full of crap. The men know I'm not.

The leading man in this story is a familiar one. He has been married for 14 years, has three kids – 13, 11, and nine – and he lives in a rat race of work, relatives, friends, home maintenance, and weekend soccer tournaments.

Sure, his sex life could be better. He wishes it were better. He might even sneak a peek at porn sites every now and then. But that's not what he longs for in his heart. It isn't the loss of sexual intimacy that causes his quiet tears.

It's the loss of his emotional and sensual connection with his only romantic partner in life. He craves her presence, respect, and trust. She is the only woman who has the power to lift him up and make him want to conquer the world for her.

Yet, he feels that she no longer wants to be that woman for him. She is disconnected. She gives herself and her energy to just about anyone but him. And it makes him sad. It makes him fearful of his future. His sadness and fear show as anger that can lead to behavior that feels neglectful and abusive to her.

The Truth Behind His Anger

Anger of this type is a secondary emotion. It is a reaction to the thoughts of what he believes he has lost and of the fear of where he thinks he will wind up. His confidence wanes, and he yields to his worst fears – that maybe he really is an inadequate and insignificant man.

The dream of "happily ever after" for most men includes the idea of a long-term, committed, romantic, and sexual relationship with a woman who shares his values and desire to maintain a healthy, trusting, respectful, and intimate relationship. The dream is full of good feelings, happy times, supportive words, and loving actions.

For many men, it feels like this dream is dying right in front of them and there is no way to stop it. Everything he does to address it seems to blow up in his face.

Can he be more understanding? Can he be more caring and sensitive? Can he take more responsibility for helping her feel safer and supportive? Yep.

He's worked hard at being a better man and husband for the last year. He's not perfect, but he's trying so hard. His wife has noticed, but she still doesn't trust him.

He wants to be a man who he can be proud of. He also wants a woman who is proud of him and appreciates him. All he needs to keep going most days is a good head scratch and a loving vote of confidence.

Author's Closing Thoughts

WHERE DO YOU GO FROM HERE?

> "The greatest help is self-help; there is no other help but self-help – doing one's best, dedicating oneself wholeheartedly to a given task, which happens to have no end but is an ongoing process."
> ~BRUCE LEE

When it comes to creating personal change, self-help books have a real short "half-life." By that I mean the insights, tools, and motivation you gain from reading them decay in just days. That's why the self-help industry is so profitable. It's like an addictive drug. You load up on one book to get the high you need and then you crash. You need another fix.

The cycle becomes self-fulfilling. The end in mind is simply to get another fix – but not to actually make any changes which could immediately transform your current reality.

In fact, taking action can feel so scary that we distract ourselves (and fool ourselves) that we are "doing the work" just because we're reading books.

The truth is that most people never do the work. Most people would rather read 50 books before actually implementing what they learned in the first one. Implementation and action always create more change in your life than planning ever will.

So, where do you go from here?

I think the best thing you can do is to make the non-negotiable choice to do something different today. You can become a different person in the next eight hours if you can muster the courage to take action.

The stories clients tell me are amazing. When they decide to make just one small change in how they respond at home or work, things magically improve. They go from a cycle of fighting in the kitchen each night to a pattern of cuddling and laughing. They go from the frustration of feeling powerless to the confidence of asking for what they want.

This is how you create the personal power and confidence you need to create the partnerships and passionate life you want.

That's where you go next.

A little less talk and lot more action!

If you want the personal guidance and mentorship of men who can support your self-help journey, encourage you each step of the way, and celebrate your amazing results with you, then visit the **Goodguys2Greatmen.com** website to establish a connection.

Mentors have changed – and continue to change my life in exponential ways. The same will be true for you. I'm anxious to meet you and hear your story.

With tons of love and respect,

Steve Horsmon

How A Tribe Of Men Saved My Life (And How It Just Might Save Yours)

I don't want to be overly dramatic here.

I can't stand it when people manufacture false drama for the purpose of making a point or selling something.

Death was not on my doorstep. My life was not in danger.

It just felt that way.

I was just another dude. It was just another divorce.

Another unhappy wife, confused husband, and a debilitating daily dose of thoughts and fears which kept me awake every night.

So, when I say a tribe of men saved my life I should probably say, **"A tribe of men showed me a new way of life."**

By the time the mention of divorce winds up on your doorstep you've probably already adopted a lot of bad habits, routines, and a rhythm of how you live your life.

This rhythm often includes a backbeat of **ineffective thinking** that leads to a nagging sense of "under performance."

It is this ineffective thinking that leads to feelings of restlessness, irritability, and anxiety.

These feelings are trying to tell you something.

They are telling you there is something more you could be doing to change your life.

And THAT can bring more tension because you just don't know what that thing is!

For me, that thing was joining a community of like-minded men who felt the same way. We ALL had similar feelings and experiences that immediately made me feel at home. Tension drained from my body.

At first, it felt like we were in the "Land of Misfit Men," because there were only about 20 of us. I still thought I was in a freak show of men who loved sharing stories, connecting deeply, displaying vulnerabilities, and discussing intellectual notions about women, sex, and relationships.

This was my tribe. My little, itty-bitty tribe.

And that's when my life changed.

After I created my Goodguys2Greatmen business and community it became clear there are millions of these men hiding in self-made caves of isolation around the world.

They have now come out into the light ... squinting in the glow of brotherly love and acceptance.

They are stretching themselves emotionally, intellectually, and spiritually in our community. It's the safest place for men to share their feelings and stories. Most stay for years as they grow, make lifelong friends, and support new members who join every day.

I still remember, after I found my tribe, the first time I cried alone as I looked into my computer screen. It was a good kind of hurt. I knew this was the missing link.

If any of this resonates with you, then maybe you're looking for your tribe.

I want to invite you to join mine.

Why? Because if you've already read this far in this obscure little book, then, brother, you've already found your tribe.

How Do You Get Involved?

Here are three ways to immediately enter the brotherhood!

1. Fill out our contact form at **goodguys2greatmen.com** (https://goodguys2greatmen.com/apply-now/) for a free 90-minute consultation with me or one of my certified GG2GM coaches. **This is a not a sales pitch**. It's a deep dive coaching session to find out what's happening, what you want, and what you may need. **Many men say they get more from this 90 minute session than they have gotten from 12 months of therapy!**

2. Join us in the **Goodguys2Greatmen Live Coaching Roundtable** (https://goodguys2greatmen.com/goodguys2greatmen-live-coaching-roundtable/). We have a secret Facebook forum and two live group coaching calls per month. This subscription can be started and stopped anytime you feel like it. **The roundtable is an extremely active and powerful tribe of men who will immediately welcome you with open arms.**

3. If you're facing separation or divorce, the **How to Defuse the Divorce Bomb** (https://howtodefusethedivorcebomb.com/) online course may be a perfect fit. This eight-hour video coaching course is a "deep, dark, and funny" dive into the reasons your wife might say, "I love you but I'm not in love with you anymore." This also includes access to the secret Facebook forum and live coaching calls with the tribe. In this tribe you'll meet amazing men in the same boat who are making courageous decisions to improve themselves and their marriage. And if divorce is unavoidable, you'll find out that there is an incredible life of confidence, strength, and hope waiting for you.

GOODGUYS 2 GREATMEN

TRANSFORM YOUR RELATIONSHIPS - BECOME THE MAN YOU WERE MEANT TO BE!

Printed in Great Britain
by Amazon